Conquering
The Canadian Death Race

By

Michael B Wentz
10/27/10

Edited

By

Izabella Wentz
Karen Wentz
Robert Wentz

Dedication

I would like to thank a few people who were instrumental in my quest for conquering The Canadian Death Race and who also helped me in completing my first book, which took me considerably longer than I expected. I only wish that I had access to something like this when I started my training. It would have saved me a tremendous amount of time.

First and foremost, I would like to thank my wife, Izabella who put up with my endless hours of training, supported me throughout the race, and helped with the editing of this book.

Second, I am grateful to my sister Katy Wentz and her boyfriend JD McPherson who helped as my crew throughout the entire race. Katy, I absolutely loved the signs that you made and the effort you put forth.

I also wish to thank you to my mother and father, Karen and Robert Wentz for their help and support with the editing of this book. And I am absolutely beholden to my three sisters, Katy, Taylor, and Missy, who have believed in me from the beginning.

Finally, I would like to thank Michael Winnemuller and Stefan Czapalay, two fellow death racers who I have become good friends with over the training process. Both helped me tremendously along the way.

"Run when you can, walk if you have to, crawl if you must; just never give up." - Dean Karnazes

DISCLAIMER: Please take this training manual with a grain of salt and adapt accordingly. What works for one individual may not always work for another.

Additionally, please excuse any spelling or grammatical errors. I tried my best to omit, as many as, possible but due to time constraints and limited access to labor, you will likely find a few mistakes.

Lastly, if you have any suggestions I would certainly love to hear of them. I will revise next year's addition to include additional training material.

Contact Information: Michael.Wentz@gmail.com

TABLE OF CONTENTS

**The Prologue is a chronicle of my Canadian Death Race experience. You can either read about my adventure below or skip to Chapter 1 to quickly get started in your own quest to completing The Canadian Death Race.

PROLOGUE

MY CANADIAN DEATH RACE STORY
By Michael Bryan Wentz

The thought of participating in The Canadian Death race started off as a bet amongst three friends. As time passed, two dropped out leaving me alone in my quest to run the 125 kilometers through the Canadian Rockies. How nice of them! My quest soon turned into obsession.

I decided that my training would start at the beginning of August 2009, about one year in advance of the 2010 Canadian Death Race. My training started off strong and the mileage picked up faster than I anticipated. This strong start lasted until four weeks later when I was bed ridden with a nasty chest infection. Too much; too fast! The infection lasted almost three weeks, negating any gains that I strived so hard for in the last month. And to top it all off my wife and I moved to a new home, which threw my training off track even further. In short, my pursuit of The Canadian Death Race was derailed until January 1, 2010.

New Year's day would mark the start of a seven-month journey towards a goal I didn't think was possible. It didn't help that I started my first day of training hung over! Nonetheless, I dragged my beaten body out of bed and slogged through my first eight tough miles. Surprisingly, by the end of this run, I felt alive again!

Everyday a little voice inside my head kept repeating, "Work hard and you will finish." I became obsessed with this mantra and researched every aspect of the training process. I learned from past experiences and slowly built my mileage to the point where I could run back-to-back long runs with ease. Nothing could stop me now.

Fast-forward to May. My training runs took me into the mountains for hours on end. I would wake up at 4 a.m. and finish at 1 p.m. My wife was none to pleased. I tried to explain, "That the training was necessary," but nothing I said could convince her that my reasoning was anything but sane. She started to worry and for good reason. Many of the runs were spent on remote mountain paths smattered with rattlesnakes and other hazardous obstacles.

She questioned my motive when I came home scraped up from head to toe. I had just fallen 10 feet down a rock littered hill after tripping on one of my poles. Several days later, my face started to swell. Apparently, I slid head first into some poison ivy. I woke up the next morning and couldn't open my eyes. I was having an allergic reaction. I was off to the Emergency Room. I had not anticipated so many unusual and unsettling setbacks.

Over 7 months of training, I went through several ups and downs. Good runs and bad runs. I experienced many mornings of injury and soreness. I would read shoe and gear reviews religiously. On any given week, I was running 60 to 90 miles a week. My obsession was bordering on insanity.

Finally, the last month arrived and my taper started. My wife was happy to have her husband home again! Now came the meticulous research. I pored through Facebook and other ultra marathon websites looking for any edge possible. I spent hours upon hours devising my race strategy and making lists of everything needed for the race. I went as far to create a "Canadian Death Race Notebook" that I carried with me everywhere I went. I then copied the notebook for each of my crew.

A week before the race, my wife and I flew first class to Chicago and then on to Calgary. When we arrived in Calgary, my sister Katy picked us up from the airport. This was the first time I had seen her in 3 years. We spent the first night at her house and the next day was spent gathering food and other gear that I couldn't bring from the States. I could barely stand the excitement. I felt so alive.

Before I had planned on running the Canadian Death Race, I promised my wife that we would make a vacation out of it. We stayed a night in Banff at the Fairmont Banff Springs Hotel and received massages, which were out of this world. We spent hours in the spa and also took the time to ride the gondola up one of the mountains. The views were breathtaking. We then dined on Fondue at the Grizzly Bear, where I loaded up on protein and carbohydrates before going into the race.

The next day, we joined my sister and her boyfriend, JD, for a 5-hour car ride through Jasper National Park. The mountain peaks were absolutely some of the tallest I had ever driven through. I highly recommend seeing them. I couldn't believe that my mission to complete the Canadian Death Race would include me seeing such spectacular sites. They were unexpected and amazing!

We finally reached Grande Cache slightly after lunch and I could hardly sit still. The town was filled with geared out runners walking around the town. A huge festival was ongoing near the recreation center with tents strewn everywhere and a massive stage right in the middle. It was an amusement park made for runners. The real amusements (*no pun intended*) would come the next day!

Soon after arriving, we unloaded all of our gear and headed over to the recreation center to pick up my registration packet. What a scene! Hundreds of runners ready to run through the Canadian Wilderness. I found my spot in the check in line and everything went smoothly. My race bag contained a bunch of SWAG (*Stuff We All Get*), my death race coin, and many other cool gadgets.

After finishing with registration, we strolled over to the Grande Cache hotel and ate a quick meal at the hotel restaurant (*surprisingly good*)! The grand finale was the pre-race meeting where race founder and organizer, Dale Tuck, gave an entertaining speech and prepared us for the next day's torture!

After setting out my race day outfit and preparing all of my gear for the next morning, I hopped into bed around 9 p.m. I felt like a kid in a candy shop, which didn't help me falling asleep. I tried and tried but couldn't seem to sleep. Finally around 11 pm, I slowly drifted off, only to wake up at 3 am. What the hell!? So not fair. I tossed and turned and eventually got out of bed and grabbed some breakfast at Noelle's (*Next Door to the Grande Cache Hotel*) around 4:30 a.m. The cashier informed me that I was their first customer! Go figure. I ordered a breakfast bagel with eggs, bacon and cheese. Delicious. This town definitely surprised me with their food. I sat down in the "town theatre" (*nice and cozy*) and watched a small part of Avatar, which happened to be showing at the time. Around 5:45am I started to get sleepy and made my way back to the hotel and crashed for two hours.

My alarm sounded and I hopped out of bed anxious to get the race started. After putting on all my gear, we headed to the starting line, which was packed with runners. I was nervous. Both my wife and sister tried to calm me down. It was a blessing to have such a great support crew.

Finally, I squeezed my way into the center of the pack and tried to relax. My heart rate was unusually high. The Canadian National Anthem rang loud over the surrounding speakers and for the first time, I started to become a little emotional. My eyes watered a little. Seven long months of dedication and hard work were about to come to fruition. This is what I had been waiting for. This was my final exam!

The weather was absolutely gorgeous. Not to hot and not to cold. No rain and only a few clouds in the sky. I was ready.

The gun fired! We were off. I took it easy the first quarter mile. I looked at my Garmin and realized my pace was a little to fast. Eventually, I settled into a rhythm where I bounced along with the music from my iPod. It was finally happening. I was grinning ear to ear, but at the same time was scared to death (no pun intended) inside. Negative thoughts started running through my head. What if I missed the cutoffs? Did I go out to fast? Did I train enough? It was at this point that I decided just to have fun.

The first four miles passed with ease. That all changed as soon as I stepped off the pavement and onto the dirt path. This was my first time on the course and I didn't know what to expect. As I entered the woods of Leg 1, I couldn't help but think, "This is much steeper and much harder than I had planned for." I steadily charged ahead. One look at my heart rate changed all of that. It was holding at 160 BPM, much higher than my planned 140 BPM! My steady jog slowly turned into a brisk walk. As I trudged along, I chitchatted with some fellow runners including fellow Facebooker and friend Stefan Czapalay. After months of chatting online this was the first time we had spoken to one another. Surreal.

I charged into the first transition five minutes under my targeted time. The cowbells and whistles gave me a huge adrenaline rush. I found my crew who had followed my instructions perfectly. I remember seeing them and letting off a sigh of relief. A friendly face was just what I needed. My crew put everything out for easy access. After switching my shoes and socks and exchanging my hydration pack, I raced out of the exchange and into Leg 2.

Leg 2, considered by many to be the hardest leg, kicked my butt. I felt great going up until the altitude seemed to zap all of my energy all at once. My preparation for the Death Race didn't include any altitude training and I felt it. Then, the cramps started to come in waves. I had calf cramps, toe cramps, inner thigh cramps, and side cramps. After reaching the top of Flood Mountain, I knew that I had to get back down as quickly as possible. As I raced down to the slugfest, I couldn't believe my eyes. The trail was so steep in parts that runners were sliding down on their bum's! My first thought was "why in the hell would anyone put a trail right here." I shook my head and trudged on. More than a few times, I tripped over roots and tree logs. At one point, I stopped and thought about what I was doing to myself. A slight grin crossed my face. At that moment, I couldn't have imagined any other place I'd rather be.

You have to remember at this point, that I had never seen the course and had no idea what to expect. As I made my way up Grande, the cramps came back again along with the fatigue. Fortunately, the view from the top made it all worth it! That is until I peered down the "power line" or the trail that I was supposed to be running down. The smile on my face turned to one of shock and fear. A thought cross my mind "How do people run down this?" It was at this point in time that my poles became my saving grace. I learned how to skip along while hopping side to side; think runner meets skier! Every few minutes though, I stopped to let my quads take a breather. More than a few times, I slipped down the rocky slope only to catch myself on a root or tree. As I reached the bottom, a crowd of onlookers cheered and this gave me enough spirit to run back into town. At just about 5 hours, I finished the infamous Leg 2. Boy, was I beat.

As I sat down at the designated spot my crew had chosen, I realized just how tired my body felt. It was at this moment, the first signs of weakness showed. I had trained my mind to push the negative thoughts back and to concentrate on positives ones. I tried to concentrate on what felt good rather than what felt bad. My crew helped tremendously with this by providing encouragement. I knew that I just needed to keep moving. Ten minutes later, I was slowly trotting out of town and onto the old mine road.

Leg 3, is one of the easier, if not the easiest, legs out of the five. That being said, many have trouble with the heat and humidity. I knew that I had hit my first wall at the exchange of Leg 2 and that I needed to break through it to keep my wits about me. As I trudged along, I noticed a slight increase in my leg turnover and unconsciously realized that I was back. My pace quickened and not too much later, I was burning down the hills and making good time on the flats. Of course, I walked all of the inclines. Even the small ones! It was at this juncture; that my mind started to wonder away from the race and the trail.

The time passed with ease and I was surprised when I looked down at my GPS and noticed that I only had just a few miles to go into the Leg 3 exchange. I was making good time and was actually right on schedule. That was until; I found out from a fellow runner that Race HQ's had extended the length of Leg 3 just before the race started. Apparently, I had missed that announcement! This was my first major hiccup, as I had only brought enough water for the original distance. The strategy was to minimize the weight factor. Luckily enough, that same runner had carried extra water and was nice enough to give me some. The rules state that any runner in the race is allowed to help out a fellow racer. The water gave me what I needed to finish the leg on schedule. As I was running into the exchange, my wife bounded over and ran alongside of me (*of course not on the actual course...I didn't want to get disqualified*). What a feeling though! That's what I call spousal support.

The high that I felt coming into the exchange quickly dissipated when I realized that my crew had chosen a spot for my equipment that doubled back towards the trail I had just run. The actual length couldn't have been more than a quarter of a soccer field. It's amazing how the smallest thing upsets you after having just run 65 kilometers. Nonetheless, it was enough to throw me into a little rampage. Though, I was quick enough to realize my mistake and made an effort towards providing an apology to my crew. I sat down and quickly switched into a fresh pair of socks. My confidence at this point was high and I became careless. I made a huge mistake by carelessly eating whatever was put in front of me. I ate pretzels, brownies, gels, bananas, and candy. The result wasn't pretty.

As I marched out of the exchange and into Leg 4, my body didn't understand what was happening. My stomach wanted to digest and my mind wanted to run. The end result was a pile of my stomach contents left along the trail. On top of the upset stomach, my body simply wouldn't stay cool and I had to take little rest stops every few minutes. The hill leading up to Mt. Hamel didn't help things much. I reached the plateau and immediately started feeling better.

The next few miles seemed to roll by with ease. My mind tried to rationalize the distance that I had left to cover. It was simple math, but at this point it might as well have been advanced calculus. I gave up and kept moving forward.

The second climb up Hamel started gradually and I thought to myself, "This is manageable." I rounded a corner and peered up the mountain to see what appeared as a goat trail that switched back and forth towards the top. "No way! That can't be the path. It simply can't be." Unfortunately, it was.

It was at this point, that I ran into a fellow death racer who had run out of water. It was Jack Cook, Canadian Death Race Record Holder (which changed after this race). He had asked one of the race volunteers for a bottle of water. The volunteer politely declined.

It states in the rules that racers cannot receive help from anyone but other racers. How do you turn down Jack Cook? I hesitantly gave him one of my bottles. Fortunately, I had carried more than I needed but it did give me a cause of concern. Meeting him on the trail gave me a little adrenaline rush. It was enough to carry me up the first quarter of Mt. Hamel. It was at this point that I sat down on a rock, pulled out a sandwich and enjoyed the gorgeous Canadian Rockies. Now, that's a hard feeling to beat.

The second half leading up to the summit of Mt. Hamel proved to be a little more challenging. I managed to murmur a few curse words under my breath as I wearily made my way to the top. While taking a second to admire the view, a sharp female voice rang out behind me telling me "Drop your gear, run to the end of this path, and grab a prayer flag." She meant business! I did as I was told and upon reaching the prayer flags. I knelt over to grab one and nearly had a heart attack. About five feet away, stood a cliff that descended hundreds of feet straight down. That certainly woke me up. As I made my way back, I couldn't help but think, "What if I lost my balance?"

The descent down Mt. Hamel was not nearly as steep as that of the slugfest or the power line, but the race had already taken its toll on my body. My only goal was to get down before sunset. Light was imperative at this point. The descent was unforgiving, as it was littered with ruts and boulders. Running in the dark with a headlight would have been a huge mental hurdle that I would have had to overcome. Fortunately, I made it down at dusk and had time to spare before reaching the next aid station.

As I reached the Ambler Loop Aid station, it was enticing to sit down, chat with the race organizers, and delay the inevitable. Anything to take my mind off of what was to come. As I refilled my water bottles, I quickly did an analysis of how my body was holding up and was surprised to find that there were no "real" problems. I mounted my headlamp and forced myself to move quickly out of the aid station. The dark gravel road before me was pitch dark and eerie. At this point in the race, my body was beyond the point of being scared. I remember thinking if something did come out and grab me, "What could I do?" The best I could manage to do was to move forward at a very slow jog. To pass the time, I partnered up with a relay runner. She was a nurse from Canada and her conversation helped lift my spirits. The loop didn't take long and soon I was back at the aid station I had just left from. It was at this point that things went from great to just plain bad.

As I took off out of the Ambler Loop Aid station and towards the next transition, my headlamp stopped working. Fortunately, course rules state that you must carry an additional light in case of something like this. I brought two small MAG lights and extra headlamp to be safe. While running, I dropped one of the MAG lights and didn't have the patience to go back and look for it. Then the second headlamp battery simply died. That left me with one little handheld MAG light. Not ideal. I still had a good 7 kilometers to go until the next exchange. Fortunately, most of it was on a flat gravel road. I kept on moving forward until I felt a burning sensation in one of my hands. It was the MAG light. Apparently, those things get hot, really hot! Now, I was tossing it from hand to hand every minute or so to alleviate the heat. To make matters worse the light started to dim a little. The extra heat was draining the battery much to fast. Fear struck at this point. I looked around and analyzed my current situation.

Here I was, in the middle of the Canadian Rockies, running in the middle of the night. I made the decision to conserve the light in case I "really" needed it. I remember reading an article about night vision at some point in my training. I closed my eyes in the dark for a minute or so and tried to adjust my eyes to the darkness. The moon, although not full, dimly lit the path and provided enough light to continue. I was frustrated, tired, and beaten, but it was working!

A second option presented itself when a relay runner started to pass me. I decided to kick it up a gear and tried to keep pace. The idea was to use his light as a guide for my own running path. It worked for a while and I made good time, but eventually I had to drop off. He was simply moving to fast for my own good. I utilized this strategy a few different times before deciding that my MAG light would be able to provide enough power to reach the next aid station where I had extra lights. As wimpy as the light was, it did the trick. During the last stretch of Leg 4, my emotions got the better of me. I was really doing this!

Onlookers, volunteers and race organizers lined the trail coming into the exchange. Whistles, cheers, and words of encouragement were shouted as I headed into the aid station. My legs felt as light as air, my heart swelled, and my eyes started to get watery. I heard loud cheers and whistles from my crowd. I looked towards the crowd and saw my crew. I saw the pride in their eyes. They were happy to see me and I was elated to see them. I reached the transition ahead of plan. I had just completed over seven hours of running. Only 24 kilometers left!

While sitting at the aid station, I switched into new socks and decided to finish the race with the road running shoes. The added cushion helped ease the pain in my already swollen feet. I grabbed an extra headlamp that I had purposely bought for Leg 5 and gorged myself with caffeine and energy gels. It was at this point that I couldn't help but notice that my mind was sharp and alert after 17 hours of running. My body, on the other hand, was a totally different story.

I bounded off into Leg 5 leaving my crew and the crowd of onlookers behind me. That bounding stride soon turned into a crawling climb, as I scrambled up a steep embankment that led into the woods. A voice yelped out behind me. I turned to find a relay runner scrambling up the bank after me. She asked me "Do you mind if I partner up with you?" Not one to decline company at this point, I said "of course." We headed into the dark together and I let her lead the way. Her company proved to be a huge advantage at this point. First, the conversation was a nice distraction from the pain my feet and legs were experiencing. Second, she hit just about every root and rock on the trail before I did, thereby, alerting me to what was to come. At this stage of the race, this was a huge advantage. Spraining an ankle or breaking a toe could derail me from finishing. Especially, since the trail is littered with roots, sticks, and logs.

My pace had slowed considerably to a brisk walk with spurts of running. I concentrated on simply putting one foot in front of the other and nothing else. Everything seemed to hurt at this point. I reached the final aid station and grabbed a glass of Gatorade and a few energy gels. Soon after, I descended into Hell's Gate, where I proceeded to hand my death race coin to the ferryman. The small boat ferried my running partner across a swiftly flowing river and onto an embankment of rocks. The drop down of the boat must have been a good four feet. It doesn't seem like much, but after the beating my legs had just taken, it felt as if I had just jumped off the roof of a house. As I landed, I winced in pain.

The second half of Leg 5 proved to be the most difficult. Not because of the terrain, but because of the state my body and mind were in. My running partner became confident with her night running ability and took off down the trail, leaving my alone in the forest. No longer could I run. I walked alone, letting the cool night air dry the sweat from my face. Walking alone left me with only my thoughts and I admired the state of mind that I was in. I had pushed my body and mind to the brink of collapse and had proved to myself that I was capable of anything. I would walk away from this race a different man from the one that had started. I took a deep breath, puffed out my chest and began to run. I eventually caught up with my friend. Another runner eventually joined us. His name was Bill Jordan and he was also running the race solo. I made an effort to stick with her and Bill until the finish.

The three of us were in high spirits as we exited the woods onto the paved road heading back into Grande Cache. As we headed into town, we all broke out into a run. It was now very early in the morning but the sun had not risen just yet. My wife, my sister, and her boyfriend were situated about 100 meters from the finish. They whooped and cheered with all their might. I sprinted towards the finish, forgetting that I had just run 125 kilometers through some of the toughest terrain. My legs felt nothing and the pain was no longer. I crossed that finish line with hands held high. I doubled over, not in pain, but in relief. My wife and sister came up to congratulate me.

I had spent 7 months training, day in and day out, and it all culminated into one single point in time. I was tired and beat, but still standing. What a moment!

I finished in 20:51:56. Good enough for a 59th place finish of 418 racers.

The high I was on was short lived. The pain returned and walking only a few short steps became a task. I had nothing left. First things first, I walked directly over to the hamburger stand and devoured that morsel like a starved wolf.

Back at the hotel, I filled the bathtub with ice and eased my body into the icy cold water. It felt strangely good. The moment alone gave me the chance to think back over what I had just accomplished. As I sat in the tub shivering, I simply couldn't grasp what I had just done.

I slept well that night. Better than I had in along time. Not because I was tired, sore and beaten. I slept because I was satisfied. My life couldn't have been better!

The next day, I accepted my award medal with pride. I walked away from Grande Cache that day a changed man.

The End And The Beginning …

Chapter 1

Introduction

"It's very hard in the beginning to understand that the whole idea is not to beat other runners. Eventually you learn that the competition is against the little voice inside you that wants you to quit." – George Sheehan.

The Canadian Death Race, to put it bluntly, is one of Canada's toughest running races - if not the toughest. The course traverses 125 kilometers over three mountain summits with approximately 17,000 feet of elevation change and one major river crossing. You likely already know this, as it's on the website and on every race poster. But, did you know everything in between those summits isn't any easier? That's 125 kilometers of hard-core terrain! Scared yet? If the name doesn't scare you, what about the race slogan "It's a killer" or the fact that there is a skull on the poster. No?! Well, you probably should be!

The race is very simple. You finish under the 24-hour cut off and you win! You win a shiny silver death race coin and more importantly, the bragging rights. It's not just any coin though. If you happen to be one of the lucky souls to finish, this coin will represent hundreds of hours of preparation, training, sacrifice, and hard work.

This book, although aimed at soloists, is useful to a relay runner or a relay team, as well. It will take you through, step by step, on what it takes to finish the Canadian Death Race. Are you ready to take on the challenge? Are you tough enough to complete this journey of hardship and suffering? Only the strongest will survive and reign victorious. Will you be one of them?

Registration opens, January 1st, on New Year's Eve at Midnight. For those of you who are unable to register, all is not lost. There is a lottery system!

The lottery system accepts entries through April 1st. It is for both solo and relay runners, alike. Once the lottery is closed, a random drawing takes place and the winners will be notified and each has 10 days to accept the invitation and to complete payment for their full entry. The website (*www.canadiandeathrace.com*) will highlight the terms and conditions for further clarity.

Chapter 2

How To Complete The Canadian Death Race

"Pain is weakness leaving your body." - Marine Corps

Are you ready for an epic journey to hell and back? Are you looking for something to prove? Are you crazy and insane? Did you read the race description? Chances are the answers to these questions are probably YES! The Canadian Death Race is not for the level headed, or is it? Whatever your answers may be, this race requires 110% commitment, dedication, and hard work. In past years, many have failed while a select few have reaped the rewards of completing the infamous Canadian Death Race. In the past two years, only 34% have finished the race solo each year! Two of every three racers around you will either drop out or not even show up. What is your destiny? Will you be the racer being dragged down from the top of Hamel or will you be the racer crossing the finish line with a big smile and your arms raised above your head? Believe it or not, most death racers don't fail because they weren't properly trained. They failed because they weren't properly prepared. Yes, there is a difference! Don't show up to the starting line without the proper preparation. Make sure every "t" is crossed and each "i" is dotted.

Whatever the reason you have for signing up, it had better be a good one because this ultra marathon isn't for the faint of heart. It requires much more than the standard training needed to complete most ultra's. Be prepared to sacrifice. Be prepared to commit, fully and wholly. And most of all be prepared to work your butt off. Do not take this race lightly. Many experienced racers have succumbed to defeat and others come back year after year failing to finish time and time again. This is a journey and it is a long one. In some cases, years are spent in preparation. It all depends on your current fitness level and your experience in running ultras. Also, a little good luck goes a long way. Whatever length of time you chose to commit is your prerogative, but MOST runners, with exception to the elite, will spend a solid 7 to 12 months in preparation - both physically and mentally.

Before we go any further let's touch upon some urgent matters. If you plan on staying at a hotel in Grande Cache make your hotel reservations pronto! You will find more information on hotels in Chapter 6.

Chapter 3

Why Listen To Me?

"Pain is temporary; finishing is forever." – Anonymous

Some of you are likely wondering why should I listen to this guy?! Where is his credibility? In all honesty, I have run the Canadian Death Race only once, but I finished under 21 hours without ever seeing the course and with my longest training run being 30 miles long. I am not an elite runner, I live at sea level, and I only spent seven months training specifically for the race. I finished 59th out of 418 solo racers, which put me in the top 15% of all finishers. At the time, I had only finished one other ultra of 50 miles (*the North Face Challenge in San Francisco a year prior*) and one official marathon (*the LA Marathon - which I completed during my training*). That being said, the most important aspect of my race preparation was the meticulous research and planning that I put in to get myself ready. I think my race result in this race speaks for itself. So, why would you take my advice? I am quite sure that most of you that are reading this are likely not elite runners, but are runners more like myself. It is my thinking that most of you will likely benefit more from the advice and experience of a runner that is more like yourself.

Chapter 4

Where Do I Start?

"The greatest pleasure in life, is doing the things people say we cannot do." – Walter Bagehot

For all intensive purposes, let's assume that you have never completed an ultra marathon. Let's assume that you are starting from scratch. In fact, let's assume you have never done any research on how to attempt a feat such as the Canadian Death Race. If this is the case, then this book will help you! Anyone can ready themselves for this race with enough time and dedication. Start as early as you can and with the right attitude, you will finish! The training program you will institute will start January 1st, so you still have plenty of time to build up your running base as much as possible.

In developing a training program for the Canadian Death Race, it is first helpful to look at the reasons why runners FAIL to make it to the finish line.

The most common reasons are:

1) Heat and dehydration
2) Dead Quads
3) Nausea and vomiting
4) Out of gas
5) Altitude problems

Let's examine these one at time and include in each section what to do and what not to do.

Heat and dehydration

This is by far the most common reason for "DNFs" (Did Not Finish) at the Canadian Death Race. Dehydration is what usually causes runners to miss the cutoffs on Leg 3. Grande Cache can by very hot and humid when the race is run at the beginning of August. The average high temperature in Grande Cache at this time of year is 19 degrees Celsius (66 degrees Fahrenheit). The record highs are 31 degrees Celsius (88 degrees Fahrenheit). You will be in the sun for extended times, which adds to what the temperature feels like. One indication of how you are doing is by making sure that you feel the need to urinate every 2 hours or so and the color should be light to clear. Maintaining the proper electrolyte balance is also important in getting to the finish line. Too few salts and you run the risk of cramping. Too many salts and you run the risk of weight gain and bloating, which could result in your body not being able to process fluids.

Dead Quads

The Canadian Death race has many extended downhill stretches where you could be running downhill for an hour or more. As we will discuss later in the downhill section of this book, the downhills are very abusive to the quadriceps muscles. Most of the abuse will be taken on leg 2, while leg 3 is the easiest and the descent on leg 4 is relatively gentle.

Nausea

Nausea is often the way the body protects itself in extreme situations. When the body experiences high levels of stress it automatically starts shutting certain systems down, one of which, is the gastrointestinal tract. As you continue to run, your muscles are calling for more fluids and energy but your system is rejecting it. Eventually, all that non-digested food comes back up. The good news is that there are ways to counter this food rejection.

*Hint:
> Try extra salt
> Suck on ice chips
> Eat something bland
> Try carbonated sodas
> Also, burping is a good sign that your stomach is working again

Running Out of Gas
This is an issue that can be resolved relatively quickly. There will be times where you just don't have much energy and is reflective of low blood sugar. It can be remedied by eating and drinking but beware as any simple sugars could result in a crash later on.

*Hint: try a combination of quick energy (simple sugars) and some longer lasting foods (complex carbohydrates)

Altitude Problems
Relatively few runners will report any "real" problems at the Canadian Death Race. That being said, you will feel tired on the mountain peaks and will likely cramp easier.

*Hint: don't idle at the top. Get down quickly and safely. You will feel your energy return once you do.

Before we move on, you have to also look at the type of race you will be running in. The Canadian Death Race is unlike most Ultras. Not because of the distance, elevation change, limited aid stations, or even the weather. Don't get me wrong, the CDR is also unique in these areas, but this specific ultra is unique due to the time cutoffs. Rarely do ultra marathons combine speed and distance together. This is the direct result of why you see so many dropouts. First, many death racers fail to toe the starting line because they believe that speed needed to be added to their workout regimen. When you combine long distance training runs and speed, you get injuries, over training, burn out, and an overused body. Secondly, at the starting line you will see soloists bursting out of the gate failing to realize the race is long. They are strong willed and persistent, but it usually gets the best of them. Why do you think such a large percentage of death racers fail to make the leg 3 cut off? It is because they went out too fast and didn't pace themselves and ran into hydration issues.

So, what does the training look like for the death race? Good question, but be patient. Before we move one let's address some items of more urgency.

Now that we have covered some of the top reasons why Death Racers fail to reach the finish, we can start to establish the costs involved and initial preparation.

Chapter 5

Costs Involved

"You gain strength, confidence and courage by every experience in which you really stop to look fear in the face." – Eleanor Roosevelt

This race can and will likely get very expensive. Looking back, I regret not keeping a log of how much I spent directly on the Death Race. Keep this in mind as you start to plan for your race. It is always interesting to look back at what your journey looked like, from start to finish. It will be very helpful to plan a budget in advance. While at the race, I overheard another racer that was not able to toe the starting line because he ran out of money. Just think of how much time that went into training and preparing! And to drop out because of funds is demoralizing. Some larger expenses to consider ahead of time include plane tickets, car rentals, hotel costs, supplements, shoes, poles, GPS watch, socks, mandatory race jacket, headlamps, water bottles, hydration pack, running clothing, compression socks, death race training camp, and indirect travel costs. Get the point?! This could easily become a multi-thousand dollar adventure! And you thought this was just running? Is your bank account ready? This list is in no way conclusive, but you get the idea. Find ways to cut corners and be prudent with your money put aside for this race.

*Hints:
> ➤ Borrow a friend's GPS watch
> ➤ Buy used poles at your local ski shop
> ➤ Use air miles for travel
> ➤ Ask other racers on Facebook to share a car ride
> ➤ Make your own supplements
> ➤ Use discount websites vs. the local running store.
> ➤ Be creative!

Chapter 6

Hotel Accommodations

"HEART is the difference between those who ATTEMPT and those who ACHIEVE. – Anonymous

It is likely as your reading this every hotel and motel in Grande Cache has already been booked for next years Race. Don't worry. Not all is lost. Call as soon as you possible and put yourself on the waiting list. Most of the hotels and motels in Grande Cache are reasonably priced, clean, and most are located only a short walk from the start/finish. Hotel rates can range anywhere from $100 to $200 per night.

*Hint:
- ➤ Put yourself on every waiting list available for every motel and hotel in Grande Cache (assuming you want one).
- ➤ Make sure you jot down the name of who you spoke to, what number you are on that list, and the date they plan on allocating hotel rooms.
- ➤ Don't fret if you do not hear back. More times than not, hotel rooms suddenly become available two weeks before the race.
- ➤ Just be sure to keep your eye on the Facebook discussions.

Grande Cache Hotels

Acorn Motel: (780-827-2412) (acorn1@telusplanet.net). Located across the parking lot from the Grande Cache hotel and within a 5-minute walk to the starting line.

Best Western: (780-827-3303 or 1-866-827-2553) - non smoking rooms and suites, full amenities, fitness center, restaurant, hot tub, high speed internet, in-room coffee/tea maker, microwave and refrigerator. Wheelchair accessible rooms available.

Big Horn Motor Inn: (780-827-3744) (bighorninn@hotmail.com) - 34 units, kitchenettes, color cable TV, telephones, laundry facilities, licensed food service, and cocktail lounge.

Grande Cache Hotel: (780-827-3377) - 48 units, kitchenettes, color cable TV, telephones, non-smoking rooms, executive suites, licensed food service, pub, cocktail lounge, and banquet facilities. About a 5-minute walk to the starting line and recreation center. Great food at the restaurant and the pub held a Victory party last year the night before the awards ceremony. Negatives: no air conditioning.

Inn on the Valley: (780-827-2453) - 48 units, kitchenettes, family suites, color cable TV, telephones, non-smoking rooms, car plug ins, courtesy coffee.

Misty Mountain Inn and Suites: (780-827-4268) - one bedroom suites, non-smoking rooms, fully equipped kitchens, in-room coffee and tea, free use of gym, onsite laundry, 24 hour camera security.

Other accommodations include the billeting program where you stay in a room with a Grande Cache family for the cost of $35/room per night for single occupancy and $45 per room per night for double occupancy. THE BILLETING PROGRAM WILL ONLY BE AVAILABLE ONCE HOTEL/MOTEL SPACE IN TOWN IS FULL

Lastly, you can also take advantage of the local campgrounds.

Grande Cache Municipal Campground: Does not accept reservations. (780-827-2404) 77 Stalls (55 full service, 22 partial service), dumping station, showers and laundry facilities. Full hook up $17/night. Partial $15/night. All sites have water and power, 55 sites also have sewage. Free fire wood, grated fire pits, picnic tables, flush toilets, showers, laundry facilities, lit roadways.

Rocky Ridge Recreation Campgrounds: Reservations are accepted. (780-827-2382, ask for Selena or Jodi), park office (780-865-5600). $20 for adults, $18 for Seniors. Pets are welcome, firewood provided, grated fire pits, picnic tables, non-flush toilets, well water. Circular loop with spacious, well treed sites. Fishing and hiking trails.

Pierre Grey's Lakes	30 km south of Grande Cache
Smoky River South	4 km north of Grande Cache
Sulphur Gates	12 km northwest of Grande Cache
Sheep Creek	25 km north of Grande Cache
Southview	45 km north of Grande Cache
Kakwa River	75 km North of Grande Cache

Chapter 7

Canadian Death Race Training Camp

"Ability is what you are capable of doing. Motivation determines what you do. Attitude determines how well you do it." – Lou Holtz

You've trained hard over the past several months and you've come a long way, but you don't want to leave anything up to chance. You're seriously considering signing up for one of the training camps. Each year, Dale Tuck, hosts several training camps to help prepare for what you are about to face. Keep your eye for sign-ups on the web page and through Facebook as space is usually limited.

Is the death race training camp a necessity? Not really. Will it help psychologically? Yes, because you will see the course and also get the chance to run portions of the course. Will it help strategically? Of course! It's a great way to learn the course and get a feel of what you will be up against. Additionally, training at altitude on the course is of huge benefit. Also, keep in mind that the trail is marked year round for training purposes. So, for those that can take advantage of the opportunity, try and get out on the trails.

If you do attend one of the camps, make sure to bring all the gear you will be training in and using in the race. It is a great chance to test your equipment in a training environment. One of the camp highlights is that you will receive instruction on how to use your poles effectively and efficiently. That being said, if you are challenged by time constrains, are strained financially, or by where you live geographically, then you can forgo the camp with an easy conscience. Many have finished the race without stepping foot on the course, including myself. Each camp takes place over the weekend and includes two training sessions per day. The camps ask that you bring a mountain bike and helmet so you can ride sections of the course and to give your legs a break. It is not mandatory that you bring the bike, as you can run the whole course. That being said, everyone that comes to the camp usually brings a bike. The camp will take you through the entire 125 kilometers of course in just 2.5 days (similar to completing three full marathons in a row ... Over mountains!). Remember the goal, at this juncture, is to see the course and mentally prepare. AND NOT GET INJURED.

Lastly, make sure to arrive at the camps fit, but well rested.

These are some recommended equipment items for the race.

Recommended Equipment List
> Moleskin, Band-Aids, duct tape
> Fanny pack or small backpack
> Hydration system (large reservoir) and/or 3 large water bottles
> High-energy food and drink
> Long lasting water proof and sweat proof sunscreen & lip balm (at 6000 to 7000 feet skin burns quite easily even on a cloudy day)
> Vaseline
> Sunglasses (anti-fog lens work best)
> Rain Gear
> Headlamp
> Night eye protection

For Running
> Running and Trail shoes (x2)
> Mountain Bike & bike helmet (everyone will be riding some of the Death Trail during the running camp, as an option).
> Sunglasses
> Minimum one spare tube & patch kit
> Mini bike pump
> Basic tools for common bike repairs (wrenches, tire iron, etc).
> Extra Batteries

Chapter 8

Three Golden Rules

"There is another type of strength. It is being able to extend your energy for a very long distance." – David LaPierre

So, you've decided, "I am going to complete The Canadian Death Race". You're filled with excitement and can't wait to start pounding out those miles. Before you strap on those new running shoes, let's first talk about you're training goals. In reading this book, if you take nothing else away, take away these three points:

First and most importantly, **DO NOT GET INJURED**. Not now, not tomorrow, and certainly not during the last month of the race.

Second, be CONSISTENT. Follow your prepared race schedule and stick to it as closely as possible. Don't forget: Nutrition, Nutrition, and Nutrition.

Third, show up to race day 100% HEALTHY. Many racers show up burned out and over trained. Don't be that Death Racer!

Follow these three goals and you will have a much higher success rate. Enough of the semantics, let's get to the details.

Chapter 9

Training Plan Overview

"The endurance athlete is the ultimate realist." – Vince Lombardi

Wow! We've covered so much material and haven't even started to talk about your training. First, you have to start thinking in terms of hours on your feet rather than miles and your training should be as specific to the race as possible. The Canadian Death Race is a trail run, with very demanding climbs and descents, usually in very warm to hot weather. The more you can mimic these conditions, the better you will be off on race day. 125 kilometers is a long way to run and there is a temptation that you must post heavy mileage in order to attempt this feat. In case you skipped over that last sentence, let me reiterate that YOU DO NOT NEED TO POST HEAVY MILEAGE TO COMPLETE THE CANADIAN DEATH RACE. Focus on quality vs. quantity and you will your improvement will be more noticeable. Everyone has their own formula, but the key is your weekly long run and possibly the addition of a back-to-back run. It is important to stress your body, but it is also important to allow it to recover again.

Your training plan will start off with a solid base. Everyone is different and every plan will differ from one another. That being said, these are some basic stages in your training. If you are familiar with those stages you can skip the next few sections and move on. That being said, it is always nice to get a quick refresher.

The Four Stages of Training:

> ➤ Developing Base Mileage
> ➤ Building Endurance
> ➤ The Mileage Ramp
> ➤ The Taper

As you read on, each stage will be addressed in detail and based on your level of training you will be able to build out your training schedule.

Chapter 10

Developing a Base (Present – March)

"If you think you won't finish, you won't." – Dick Collins

It is a good idea to start your base stage and mileage buildup, at the latest, in January then slowly increasing the time and distance on your feet during the first three months of the year. Although, starting your training in January does assume that you have some sort of base or experience in ultra running already. If you do not, it is suggested that you start building your base right now (as in today, months before January). The base phase should be last around 12 weeks and for all intensive purposes, will start January 1st.

As you likely already know, a base of training is needed before you start to target any sort of specificity training. Your workouts in the base stage should be characterized by increasing the amount of time and distance on your feet and is all about aerobic fitness. The length of your base training program depends entirely on how much time you will spend training for the CDR. Many runners will dedicate an entire year to this one race.

Whatever length of training you chose, do not increase either your (1) weekly mileage and/or (2) long run mileage by more than 10% a week. Doing so greatly increases the chances of incurring an injury, thereby delaying or stopping your training all together. If this does happen, do not fret! Don't lose sleep over taking a step back in your training. This is natural and happens to most. If it does happen, try to find a substitute for your training. That substitute can be swimming, cycling, weights, etc. It could even be mental training. Spend the time you would have been logging miles, by reviewing your race strategy. Remember, during the base training stage and any other stage for that matter, it is a good idea to get some cross training intertwined with your regular running training (i.e. yoga, cycling weights, and swimming). That does not mean you substitute your cross training with any of your scheduled runs. The cross training is meant to help strengthen other muscles and give your running muscles a break. Many runners want to spend there "days off" running and if you're going to exercise, then I suggest you substitute those days with some cycling, weight training, and/or swimming.

By January 1st, you should be running around four to five times a week with at least 50 kilometers per week and at the point where you're able to run 15 to 20 kilometers for your weekly long or every-other-week long run. You will not do any running on Monday or Friday. If you're feeling fresh and are able to exercise one of these days, then implement some sort of other cross training activity.

Most importantly, you should be running in 4-week cycles. Week 1 is your base week. Week 2 mileage should increase by 10%. In week 3, increase the distance of your long run. Week 4 is your recovery week where you return back to your base mileage. This allows for muscle recovery.

Goals of The Base Building phase

- ➤ Build cardiovascular and muscular endurance
- ➤ Increase aerobic fitness
- ➤ Increase weekly mileage
- ➤ Increase length of long run
- ➤ Improve V02 Max

A typical training program for the months of January, February, and March might look something like this.

Monday   Rest, or 45 minutes easy/bike ride/yoga/weights
Tuesday   30-45 minute run
Wednesday   1-hour run
Thursday   1-hour run
Friday   Rest
Saturday   2-hour run
Sunday   1.5-hour run

Starting January 1st, you're plan may look a little something like this. Remember, in order to be able to do the heavy work in April and May, you will need to develop a significant base January through March. Distances are in miles.

Week	Mon	Tues	Wed	Thur	Fri	Sat	Sun	Total
1	--	2	4	6	--	14	8	34
2	--	4	8	6	--	16	8	42
3	--	4	8	6	--	16	8	42
4	--	4	8	6	--	18	10	46
5	--	2	4	6	--	14	8	34
6	--	4	8	6	--	18	10	46
7	--	4	8	6	--	18	10	46
8	--	4	8	6	--	20	12	50
9	--	2	4	6	--	14	8	34
10	--	4	8	6	--	20	12	50
11	--	4	10	6	--	23	12	55
12	--	4	10	6	--	23	12	55

From this point, a longer run of increasing increments can be added. That being said, the longer you have to focus on your base the better. Remember to focus each run on QUALITY.

Chapter 11

Strength & Endurance (April – June)

"If you under-train, you may not Finish, but if you over-train, you may not start." – Tom Dubos

Starting on April 1st, you will start the strength-building phase of your program. During this phase, you will concentrate on increasing the number of muscle fibers in your leg muscles and increasing your lactate threshold. To put it simply, you will focus on getting stronger. You should start to incorporate hill training each week. Not able to run hills or don't have hills? No problem. Hike them. Hike them often and hike them aggressively. This doesn't mean running hills every day. At most, run hills on Wednesday and on the weekend. This phase should last 12 weeks.

Do not become a mileage junkie. Focus on quality versus quantity. This is not to say long runs are not important because they are. Limit your longest run in training to no more than 40 miles. Everyone is different. My longest run going into the CDR was 30 miles. Figure out what's best for you and go with it. You do not need to slog through a 50 mile run for the sake of toughening yourself. It is actually going to wear you down. You will actually get more benefit from a 30 mile run at a decent clip versus a 50 mile run at a relaxed pace. You will spend less time in training and less time beating your body to a pulp.

Goals of the Strength Building Phase

➤ Build muscle strength
➤ Improve lactate threshold
➤ Maintain Aerobic Fitness
➤ Increase VO2 max
➤ Maintain cardiovascular and muscular endurance

A typical training program for the months of April and May might look something like this.

Monday	Rest, or 45 minutes easy/bike ride/yoga
Tuesday	60-90 minutes
Wednesday	Two to three hours
Thursday	60-90 minutes
Friday	Rest
Saturday	Five to six hours on hills
Sunday	one to three hours, easy long recovery run

Starting April 1st, you're plan may look a little something like this. Distances are in miles.

Week	Mon	Tues	Wed	Thur	Fri	Sat	Sat	Total
13	--	2	4	6	--	14	8	34
14	--	4	12	6	--	25	13	60
15	--	4	12	6	--	25	13	60
16	--	4	12	6	--	25	13	60
17	--	4	8	6	--	10	8	36
18	--	4	12	6	--	28	15	65
19	--	4	12	6	--	28	15	65
20	--	4	12	6	--	28	15	65
21	--	4	8	6	--	10	8	36
22	--	4	15	6	--	30	15	70
23	--	4	15	6	--	30	15	70
24	--	4	15	6	--	30	20	75

Depending on the terrain and speed, this should give you anywhere from 60-90 miles a week. Near the end of June, it would be very beneficial to put in a longer attempt of 8 to 10 hours hiking with some intermittent running. Whatever you do, follow the golden rule and DO NOT GET HURT. Use this longer training run try to simulate will you will be doing in the Death Race. You must show total commitment. The hard part isn't the training, but the preparation required. Use your training runs as if they were races. Practice eating, drinking, changing shoes, and clothes. Do anything possible to simulate the race.

Chapter 12

Taper (July)

"Your body will argue that there is no justifiable reason to continue. Your only recourse is to call on your spirit, which unfortunately functions independently of logic." – Tim Noakes

Hopefully, you've made it thus far, injury free and all mental and physical faculties intact. The planning and preparation have paid off, but you're starting to worry, what could have I done more or is there something else that I can do? This happens to just about everyone going during the last two weeks before his or her taper.

You've now trained for months and the race is soon approaching. You can hardly stand still! Every dream, every thought, and every action revolves around the race. Every stage of your training plays an integral part in your successful completion. The taper is no different and should be viewed as essential. There are conflicting views on the taper. Some racers will profusely tell you not to taper and will train up until race day. Others view the taper as a necessity. Whichever camp you fall under, please read the following and decide for yourself what is best for you.

The taper plan will start three Saturday's before the Race where you will run the longest run of 30 to 40 miles followed by a 20 to 25 mile run. You will run 75 miles in total during this 3rd week. At this point, you will start to fortify your body with Zinc, Echinacea, Potassium (bananas, potatoes, beet greens, cantaloupes and beans), and Vitamin C.

The following week (week 2 of taper), you will reduce your mileage from 75 miles to 40 miles with 10-mile long runs on both days. Beginning one (1) week before the event bedtime is 10:00pm every night. One Saturday before the race will be a long run of 10 miles followed by no running on Sunday. Most of the runs two weeks before the race will be higher intensity and low volume runs. You will concentrate on sleeping 3 to 4 days before the race and try to get in a great nights sleep two nights before just in case you cannot sleep the night prior.

The final characteristic of a successful taper relates to the frequency of training sessions: you should reduce the total number of sessions by no more than 30%. Any further reduction may result in a decrease in performance, because you may lose the "feel" for the activity.

During the last week, try to eat a diet that is higher in proportion of carbohydrates than your normal diet. Try to eat as much good food as you can. Also, it is beneficial gain a couple pounds in that last week or so. That doesn't mean that you start frequenting the local burger shop! Eat healthy. The stored fat and carbohydrates will be put to good use during the run. Rest up and drink plenty of fluids.

The optimal pre-exercise/pre-race diet should fill your muscles with glycogen. It should be high in carbohydrate, moderate in protein, and low in fat and fiber. To achieve maximal glycogen loading, begin 1 week before competition. First 3 days: Low-carbohydrate diet to deplete muscle glycogen. Next 3 days: High-carbohydrate diet with little or no activity. This yields muscle glycogen loading with glycogen and water to prepare for the 7th day event.

THE PRE-EXERCISE MEAL:

➢ Should be eaten 2-3 hours before
➢ Small, easily digestible
➢ Familiar
➢ High in carbohydrate
➢ Does not produce gastrointestinal distress
➢ Moderate in protein, low in fat
➢ If nerves prevent intake of solids, fruit juices, sports drinks, or glycogen replacement products
➢ Should be determined while training, not the day of the event.
➢ Examples: bagels, whole wheat bread, crackers, jelly, all juices, brown/white rice, English muffins, cereal, pasta, sports drinks, apples, bananas, oranges, raisins.
➢ Make sure to try your planned pre-race meal before a long training run to see how your body handles it.

Chapter 13

Hydration

"The road to excess leads to the place of wisdom, for we can never know what is enough until we have experienced to much." – William Blake

The CDR takes place during the summer months, which means warm - and sometimes downright hot - running conditions for most death racers. Combine this with a high level of humidity and you have a recipe for disaster. The need for proper hydration is absolutely essential. Our bodies have the ability to cool themselves in the form of sweating, if and only if, the body is adequately supplied with fluids. The key is to keep our system in balance. Don't let yourself become dehydrated, and don't over-hydrate either.

A runner can sweat one to two liters per hour. Sweat rates can exceed two liters per hour under extreme conditions or for people who sweat profusely. That said, our intake is limited to approximately one liter per hour, so you can see where the importance of staying hydrated prior to the death race can be critical to performance. The key to staying hydrated is knowing your body well enough to keep your pace at a point to where you can reduce your sweat rate. Makes sense right?

Slow down, sweat less, and be able to continue running. Involved in this equation, are the types of fluids you are drinking. Fluids with carbohydrates should ideally have around 7% or 8% concentration. In addition, you should also have an adequate amount of sodium and potassium. Don't believe me? Ask almost any runner about their experience at the top of Flood on Leg 2. Ask almost any runner about cramps during any part of the death race. I heard people complaining about groin cramps, toe cramps, calf cramps, and quad cramps. You name the cramp and someone had it. On every training run, practice your fluid intake along with intake of sodium and potassium. Every runner is different, as electrolyte losses will vary by fitness and heat acclimatization.

There are several brands of salt pills on the market. Two of my favorites include: Succeed Caps (higher sodium content but harder on the stomach) and Hammer Endurolytes (lower sodium content but easier on stomach). Practice with both and see what works best for you. Most runners will need 200 to 500 mg of salt per hour, but it depends on your body and how well you are trained, as well as, how well you are adapted to the heat.

Sports drinks are plentiful, so how do you chose? In training of course! Many have had positive things to say about Hammer Perpeteum. Some stick to the old fashion Gatorade. Although, I advise against drinks such as Gatorade or Powerade. They simply don't have what you need for a really long, slow, burn and they always seemed too sugary. Either way, it is a good idea to drink both water and sports drink together. Experiment with different types of fuel too and learn what your stomach can handle while running. Other drinks developed for longer endurance events include Enervit or eLoad. The drinks will go down like water, but also give you all the energy and nutrients you need to keep going.

Chapter 14

Nutrition

"You can't die from a stomach ache. The worst that can happen is that you'll throw up. Then you can eat some more and start running again." – Jack Bristol

"If you feel like eating, eat. Let your body tell you what it wants." – Joan Benoit Samuelson

You're about to embark on one long training program and will need to focus more on nutrition than you have ever before. A well-designed nutrition plan should be the foundation of your training program. The plan should focus on meeting your energy needs and incorporating timing of nutrients to help optimize performance and enhance recovery. Ultra runners that are working out five times a week for two to three hour session will need anywhere from 2,500 to 8,000 calories! It will be difficult to maintain your high mileage and calories without a plan and that plan will makes a huge difference in your training and your race performance.

Timing of Nutrients
Try to remain consistently fueled and eat evenly throughout the day, rather than eating a few large meals. Concentrate on keeping your blood level stable and not getting hungry. Ideally, you will want more of your calories at the beginning of the day, as it takes approximately four hours for carbohydrates to be digested and begin to be stored as muscle and liver glycogen. Glycogen is your secondary long-term energy storage. If you run in the afternoon, breakfast will be the most important. Following your workout, consume protein and carbohydrates to accelerate muscle glycogen re-synthesis and storage. Protein shakes following a workout work wonders. Hammer makes a drink called Recoverite that has received favorable ratings.

Carbohydrates
Carbohydrates are the cornerstone of your diet. You will need anywhere from 6 to 10 grams/kg/day. Dense grains and nutrition products will help you consume.

Protein
Not getting enough protein in your diet can slow your recovery and over time can lead to muscle wasting and poor training tolerance. Protein is not all equal and your choices should be high quality and low in fat. Best sources are skinless chicken, fish, egg whites, and skim milk. Supplements include whey, colostrums, casein, milk proteins, and egg protein.

Fat
Unlike the increased consumption you would see in Carbohydrates and protein from increased exercise, fat should be kept at the same consistent intake.

Vitamins & Minerals
It has been demonstrated that specific vitamins may possess some health benefits for ultra runners. Vitamin C and E may help in tolerating the heavy training. Other supplements include fish oil, flax seed, etc.

Water
Use a scale to weigh yourself before and after a workout to learn your own personal sweat rate. You should drink approximately two to three glasses of water for every

pound lost on a run. Do not take water consumption lightly. It can be one of the most important things you can do for your performance.

Chapter 15

Heart Rate Monitor

"Speed and strength are of diminishing importance at greater and greater distances." – David Costill

Do you absolutely need a heart rate monitor to complete the Death Race? Absolutely not. Is it helpful? Yes. There are many benefits to using one in your training and during the race. It is helpful in providing a continuous measurement of the work and intensity level and can be used to monitor how your body responds to heat, humidity, altitude, or any other factor. Once you analyze the data you can work to respond to those issues. It is helpful to find your optimal heart rate during specific temperatures. That way, you are able to adjust accordingly on race day. This is important during the climbs on Leg 2 and with the heat on Leg 3, which both claim many souls due to over pacing and dehydration. Many runners on Leg 2 will be suffering from cramps and an even larger quantity will be walking Leg 3 due to dehydration.

The data that you collect can also be used to identify over training. If you find your heart rate is 10-15 beats higher at a running rate where you are usually lower then it could be a sign of over training. In this case, you might take a day off or two to let your body recharge. While these little devices are effective in some ways, there are some negatives. You can easily start to focus entirely on the GPS rather than how you feel. There are times in training where you need to push your body a little harder and a little longer. You might feel that the monitor actually causes you to train less.

The number of articles on how to use a heart rate monitor is lengthy and in an effort to focus on the death race we are going to simply touch upon the basics. First, you must find your Maximum Heart Rate (MHR). The simple formula is:

Maximum Heart Rate
Women: 226 - your age
Men: 220 - your age

After you find your Maximum heart rate you can figure out your target heart rate zone. Here is the simple formula: (MHR * Target %).

There are 4 heart rate zones in which to operate in:

1) Energy Efficient   (60-70%)
2) Aerobic   (70-80%)
3) Anaerobic   (80-90%)
4) Red Line   (90-100%)

Generally, you want to be between 70 and 80 percent of your heart rate or within the Aerobic stage. So, if you have a MHR of 190 then your target zone would be 133 to 152. Going below this and your not working hard enough. Going above this and your risking injury. That being said, "recovery" runs should be done at a pace below and "speed or tempo workouts" should be done at the higher end of the range or just above. Rarely, in your training should you be in the Red Line Zone.

Chapter 16

Running Downhill

"Easy to run downhill, much puffing to run up." – Chinese Proverb

Ask yourself right now, "How do I increase the probability of my success in the Death Race?" Obviously, due to the title of this chapter, the answer is on the downhills! A SIGNIFICANT portion of the death race is downhill. Inexperienced ultra runners often reply, "That's great! The downhill's are the easy part, right?" Wrong. The downhills will either be your saving grace or the final nail in your coffin. Dead quads are consistently one of the top reasons racers cite for being unable to finish an ultra.

Even though less energy is required to run down a moderately easy hill, your muscles will still be taking on stress. When you are going downhill, your anti-gravity muscles are working eccentrically. These muscles are trying to contract at the same time they are being lengthened. As you run down a hill your quads are being stretched by the force of gravity, which is pulling you down the hill. At the same time, the quads are attempting to contract to fight the force of gravity. Without getting more technical, basically, all that stress can produce a significant amount of muscle damage, especially during extended downhills, which is pretty much every downhill in the Death Race.

The most efficient way of training your "downhill" muscles is by running downhills. Does this mean foregoing squats, lunges, and weight resisting exercises?

Of course not. These exercises are essential to your performance, but should not be used as a substitute for getting out on the trails and hitting those downhills.

Herein lies the problem. Running hills to often, when your body is not ready, and/or over trained risks future injury. Remember those stages we discussed earlier in the book? You should not be doing any hills during the base stage or the taper. Additionally, your last hill training run should be done one month from the start of the race. The question arises "How do I get the necessary downhill training without risking injury and also realizing enough gains for the race? Isn't that a large chunk of training? Yes and no. Most of your heavy hill training should be done at least 2 months in advance of the race and not more than 4 months before. Most of the hills should be run during your third month. Does this mean running downhills during every run? Of course not! First and foremost, try to run hills on fresh legs to limit the risk of injury. Secondly, try to get in at least one of your long runs each week during the third month on downhills. During the second month before your race, I recommend giving your muscles a break the first week, getting one nice long run on hills in the second week, and one of your longest runs the last Saturday before the race on hill. You can refer to the schedule section for a more detailed look at a training plan.

*Hint:
> Using poles can help alleviate and/or buffer the consistent pounding on the downhills.
> Learn to skip, hop, and ski on those downhills.
> Save the quads!

No hills in the area where you live? No problem. Get creative. Find an overpass. Do repeats. Find a treadmill with a decline or find something to put under it. Do whatever you can to emulate the feeling of running downhill. It will pay dividends over and over again during the race.

And now, for the million dollar question "How do I run downhills?" As effectively and efficiently, as humanly possible. Think of yourself as a road runner with you feet spinning beneath your body and lightly tapping the ground with each hit. You should have a slight lean forward and with your arms and body balanced. Try to let your body go. It should feel effortless.

Now for the bad news. Sorry, but those death race hills are steep, steep, steep! One fellow racer named, Michael Winnemuller, told me "I don't want to scare you, but the MOUNTAINS in the CDR are tough!" I wished he had scared the crap out of me because they were much more tougher than I could ever have imagined and I trained in what we call mountains here in California. I want to scare you. I want you to be prepared. I will put this bluntly. The MOUNTAINS you will be CLIMBING and FALLING down during the CDR are much more brutal than you can imagine. No one in their right mind would train on such hills for fear of injury. If you're an inexperienced ultra runner and are running on similar terrain to that of the death race during your long runs of, let's say, 25 or 30 miles, you are over training. Your body will not be able to sustain the abuse. The death race will rip your legs off, chew them up for dinner, and spit them out. Don't believe me? Ask any other runner, that had never run the course or saw the course before the race, what their expectations where before and after.

Now that I have scared you to death, let's scare a little more! The mountains never stop coming. Yes, there are SOME flat sections, but around every bend is another mountain to climb. Sound fun yet? Oh yeah! Let me give an example to the racer who lives in a place where there are no hills. Can you hang your treadmill upside down in your house and run up or down it? Of course not, but it still wouldn't be steep enough! It's a joke, but I am only partially exaggerating.

Ok, so the hills are tough. You get it. Now what!? How do you train for a race where the training is pretty much impossible to emulate without having the course in your backyard. The answer is to find the steepest downhills and uphills in your area and run them until you your legs are quivering and shaking. Just remember the first golden rule, from the beginning of the book, "DO NOT GET INJURED!"

10 Downhill Running Tips

1) Relax and don't forget to breath
2) Scan 5 feet ahead of you (your brain is faster than you are)
3) Short strides, high turnover, and increased cadence
4) Gravity is your friend, go with it
5) Choose the correct shoes
6) Be gentle on your landings
7) Don't lean back
8) Try not to strike on your heels
9) Feel the trail as you go
10) HAVE FUN and FLY!

Chapter 17

Running Uphill

"You can never run a hill too hard, you will collapse before hurting it. – Adam born

When you sleep at night, do you dream about bounding up the mountains of the Canadian Death Race? Yes!? Well, keep dreaming. The only hill you should be running is the hill going into the finish line.

As mentioned in the downhill section, the MOUNTAINS are relentless and simply keep going up and up. They are long sustained climbs at relatively high altitudes. If you do not monitor your heart rate, your hydration intake and your sweat output carefully, you will cramp! Be prepared to deal with cramps. Know how to stretch them out and when to take salt tablets. Also, understand the faster you get back down the mountain, the less tired you will feel. Don't believe me? Ask other previous death racers. Facebook is a great place to start.

Make sure to take deep breaths and focus on getting in a rhythm. Monitor your heart rate if possible. You should try to keep your heart rate around 70% of your maximum heart rate. This will be difficult as you're using your upper body, which generates additional energy. The effort put forth on most hills should feel easy and consistent. If you do run hills, they should be done at a slow pace.

5 Uphill Running Tips

1) Elongate your stride
2) Emphasize arm action
3) Run on the tips of your feet and work your calves
4) Don't pass the redline
5) Save some energy by walking near the crest so you can run back down

*HINT: I trained for 7 months specifically for the death race and RARELY ran up the hills in my training. Yes, I hiked them aggressively with poles, but rarely ran them. Why? Running up hills puts you at risk for injury, especially, tight or pulled calves (one that I am prone to). Your heart rate is elevated and puts you in the anaerobic zone, thereby, creating lactic acid, which in effect puts you at risk for future injury. Additionally, if you're planning on finishing the death race, then your strategy, most likely, will not include ANY up hill running during the race. I walked EVERY uphill during the race and finished in under 21 hours. How? I ran the downhills efficiently. That being said, you must run some hills and you must figure out what works best for you!

Chapter 18

To Pole or Not to Pole; that is the Question

"Don't fear moving slowly forward ... fear standing still." Kathleen Harris.

Is this your first CDR? If yes, use poles. Is this your second CDR? If yes, use poles. If this is your third CDR? Then, you have the right to decide. I think you're starting to get the idea. Use poles. Use them in training and use them in the race. This doesn't mean that you will run every training run with poles. In fact, you probably won't need them until the latter half of your training. Racers new to the Death Race sometimes think that finishing with poles somehow diminishes their bragging rights or that people will think less of them. If you cross that finish line in under 24 hours, as a soloist or as a team, you will get the same medal as the guy or gal standing next to you who finished without the poles. By running without poles you will have proved nothing other than the fact that you weren't prepared, when you didn't finish under the cutoff. Some of you will say, "No, not me. I am proving that I can finish without them." Some will still finish and some won't. Either way. It's your choice.

Poles come in all different shapes and sizes. There are ski poles, hiking poles, and trekking poles. There are carbon and aluminum poles. There are poles that expand. You get the idea. The options are limitless and so is the money you can spend on them! First, decide if you want expandable poles or not. Then decide what material and what size you will need. This depends on preference. Most say that shoulder height is about right. I believe around 50 inches or so should do the trick, but it all depends on preference. Carbon is stronger, but snaps easier. Aluminum has the ability to bend but can buckle easier on weight. Many sports stores have a flexible return policy. Use this to your advantage until you find the poles that are right for you.

Everyone has their own theory and strategy on how to use the poles. Supposedly, the Death Race Training Camp teaches you how to use them. I have heard positive things about the Death Race Training Camp, but have never attended. If you have the chance, it wouldn't be a bad idea to attend. They give you an introduction on how to use the poles. That being said, use your own techniques that you have tried and perfected during training. The uphill strategy is fairly standard. When walking up hill or on flat sections, raise BOTH poles in front of you and propel your self forward. The tricky part is using poles during the downhill sections. Some racers use them purely for stability purposes while others use them as buffers. I use a move similar to that of skiing moguls. On steeper declines, I will be "skiing" down the slope. It takes pressure off the quads and puts it on the poles. This is not recommended in the race without preparation. Other times you will see me skipping down the hills with the poles used as a buffer.

Lastly, when do you start practicing with the poles? This is a great question. You don't want to lose any of the gains you would have realized from running without poles. At the same time, you must train those "pole" muscles just as you train your legs. So, my recommendation is to start incorporating your poles on one of you long runs each week around two to three months in advance of the race. It depends on how much you actually use them in your runs. You can also use the weight room or a rowing machine to workout those same muscles. Triceps and back exercises are excellent for your "pole" muscles. Whatever you use as your strategy, be sure that you are comfortable with the poles come race day!

* Hint: visit your local ski shop and ask if they have any old poles that you can purchase. I happened to pick up a carbon pair for $5. They were perfect! All that was needed was some baskets at the end. I had trouble finding them at the local sports store, so I took some Gatorade caps and cut holes in them. I used duct tape to keep them in place. They worked flawlessly!

Chapter 19

Cross Training

"The mind learns the body can go at least a bit further even though it feels increasingly uncomfortable." - Pritikin

The best advice I can give is to pick up a second sport and cross train. When you do a 40+km run one day and have been running every day leading up to that you can burn your legs out. I used cycling, and put in a good three hour-long ride once a week to take a break from running. You give your running muscles a break, but can still get a cardio workout and train mentally. Turn every daily activity into an exercise. If you sit down at a desk all day, do stomach crunches or leg lifts. Be creative.

Cross Training Activities
- Weightlifting
- Swimming
- Cycling
- Walking
- Yoga
- Pilates

Chapter 20

Night Training

"The woods are lovely dark and deep, but I have promises to keep, and miles to go before I sleep, and miles to go before I sleep." – Robert Frost

When the sun goes down, so will your spirit. The darkness can and will suck the life right out of you. Your mind must take full control because your body wants to sleep. Allowing your mind to overcome the body will help you persevere throughout the nighttime hours. Think about what it is that motivated you to attempt to run the distance in the first place.

If you don't have any experience on trails at night, try a few trial runs. Are you scared? It's natural and expected. By the time you reach darkness in the race, as a soloist, you won't care. You're tired and beat. Part of you will probably wish that boogieman would come out and grab you to end your misery! That being said, practice with you headlamps and/or flashlights. Test the batteries and lamps. Get an idea of how long they last and how strong they are. Most sports stores have a flexible return policy. Find which works best for you and then try to find discounts online. Whatever you do, make sure you have a reliable back up light and batteries.

Chapter 21

Train The Brain

"Laziness is nothing more than the habit of resting before you get tired." – Jules Renard

No pain, no gain! Every runner, experiences some sort of pain during the race - even the elite. The physical training for an ultra is obviously important, but the mental side is just as important, if not more. You can command your body to perform no matter the pain. It takes determination, desire, and the willingness to push yourself. Prepare yourself mentally by knowing that you will feel awful, but that pain will go away, only to feel bad again. It's a matter of how much you want it and if you don't have the desire the pain will become your main focus. Run when you can and walk when need, but always stay moving and eventually you will cross the finish line.

5 Tips
1) Focus attention on moving forward.
2) Baby Steps. Take it mile by mile rather than looking at the entire distance.
3) You can't allow pain or distance to overwhelm you.
4) Run from tree to tree and then walk from tree to tree.
5) Try your best late in the race to incorporate at least a minimal amount of running at all times.

*Hint: If you allow yourself to walk for a significant period of time the death march will begin. The best way to stop the death march is to breathe deeply, remove any negative thoughts, and start to shuffle your feet. A slow shuffle will loosen the muscles and eventually allow you to run freely again.

Chapter 22

Altitude

"If you start to feel good during an ultra, don't worry you will get over it." Gene Thibeault

The effects on altitude performance are important to look at when considering your course strategy. The higher you go, the less oxygen you will have available for the body to use. You either need to adapt to the lack of oxygen at these heights by living and training at altitude or slow your pace down significantly. It is important to conserve your energy early on because altitude can and will sap your energy until you get back to comfortable altitude levels. Let's face it, it's not likely that you're going to have the time or funds to train and live in Grande Cache for several weeks before the race. Most of us are coming in a day or two ahead of time. If you are able to arrive a few days in advance you should perfectly fine. Just make sure to monitor your body closely and slow down if necessary. Remain in your lactate threshold or you may never see the finish line. Step to the side of the trail and take a rest when you're tired. Don't feel bad as runners pass you. Some are relay runners. The others are the solo runners who you will be playing a game of seesaw with for the rest of the race.

Chapter 23

Injuries

"My doctor told me that jogging could add years to my life. I think he was right. I feel ten years older already." - Milton Berle

Oh, the agony! Tight Hamstrings, IT Bands, and Calves will put you sidelines. Plantar Fasciitis, Heel Bursitis, and Achilles Tendonitis can derail your training. Sprained ankles pulled hamstrings, and knee problems can be debilitating. The answer is to prevent, prevent, prevent. Know your body and the instant you feel something out of sort, STOP. You're body is trying to tell you something!

Ultra marathon newbie's always believe that missing one or two training sessions will set them back more than it actually does. They fret and worry about losing all the gains they have achieved. They fail to realize that one, two, or even three days will have little effect on their training. More times than not it actually is of more benefit. Rest is essential.

The Feet (Blisters and Black Toes)

Running 125 kilometers over 17,000 feet of elevation takes a big toll on your feet. Take care of them and they will take care of you. You will be trekking through water, mud, and rocks, all of which, could lead to a DNF. All of this combined with sweat creates the perfect recipe for blisters. Once you feel a hot spot develop, immediately take care of it. Carry a few band-aids, some moleskin, duct tape, and body glide. Taking an extra minute or two on the side of the trail might affect your finishing time, but not addressing them until it's to late could cause a DNF.

There is not much you can do for black toes once the damage is done. Try to find shoes that are big enough to accommodate the movement of the foot while running down hill. Also, keep your shoelaces tight, but make sure they are not to tight. Tight shoelaces can cause a host of other problems.

Chafing

You definitely don't want to be the one running down Mt. Hamel looking like you're on an invisible horse. Chafing is one of the most uncomfortable feelings a runner can experience. There is nothing worse than you're skin being rubbed off by other skin and knowing it's happening. Put Band-Aids on your nipples to prevent rubbing and put lubricant on areas prone to rubbing. Prevent chafing by wearing shorts you know have worked in training and by carrying one of the products below at all times.

Bag Balm is designed for cow udders and stays on way longer than Vaseline. Additionally, it contains some healing properties.

Desitin is used primarily for healing not as prevention. Consider using after the race.

Vaseline - make sure you buy the petroleum base. It lasts the longest.

Body glide is sold in most running stores and is a deodorant sized container making it easy for carrying.

Chapter 24

Gear Suggestions

"The general who wins the battle makes many calculations in his temple before the battle is fought. The general who loses makes but a few calculations beforehand." – Sun Tzu

Headlamp
The difference between an "ok" headlamp and an "great" headlamp is much more than just added light. Don't skimp on buying a lower cost headlamp. Unless you're part of the elite, you will likely be running at least a good 5 to 7 hours in the dark. That being said, there are "lesser known" brands with just as much output than there competitors. Most decent lights will run anywhere from $60 to $150. Keep in mind that some are heavier due to the battery weight, where as, others might not last quite as long lasting. My suggestion is to have two headlamps; one on your head and one on your waist, as it takes away the depth perception problems.

Running leg 5 (mostly single track) is hard on the eyes. You can't really take your eyes off for a second.

*Hint: find a relay runner that you can stick with on Leg 5 and use them as a guide. They will hit every root and stick for you along the way. After running as long as

you have, any relief where you don't have to concentrate is welcoming. At times I would hear someone swear out loud from hitting his or her toes. Lastly, look for the florescent dots on the trees to guide your way.

Headlamp Recommendations:
- Surefire Minimus
- Zebra H50
- FenixHP10
- Princeton Tec
- Night Runner Belt
- Petzl MYO XP

Shoes

Pick your shoes carefully. Different shoes have different support characteristics and having the wrong type of shoe can lead to injury. Your best chance of finding the perfect pair is to first find a local running store that will analyze your gait or running form. In short, they can tell you if you are a pronator, supinator, or neutral runner and also if you have high, low, or neutral arches. Second, give them a try indoors and see if they have "the feel".

You should also consider having multiple pair of shoes for different legs of the race. Everyone has their own preferences, but the consensus is that you should have technical shoes with support for legs 2 and 4, and trail shoes for legs 1,3, & 5. As the miles wear on, your feet can become tired in parts where the shoes aren't as supportive. By switching to a different pair of shoes, you can give the stressed areas of your feet a break by shifting the support areas with a different shoe. The dynamics can be different from one shoe to the next in terms of heel lift, forefoot flexibility, arch, traction, etc. This in effect, not only gives relief to your feet but your knees, ankles, hips, and even lower back. Changing shoes during a run can have a similar effect of feeling like you have a new pair of legs or feet. Shoes also lose some of there shock absorption and that absorption takes about 48 hours to recover, so rotating shoes might be helpful. It's best to have at least 3 pairs just in case the conditions are wet and muddy. That being said, don't change the shoes if they are working. If it ain't broke, don't fix it.

Trail Shoe Favorites:
- ➢ Salomon
- ➢ Montrail
- ➢ Brooks
- ➢ Asics

Road Shoe Favorites:
- ➢ Asics
- ➢ Brooks

Socks

Socks are socks, right? Wrong. Socks are a way to save a few bucks? Wrong. Picking the perfect sock just might be the difference between, you reaching the finishing line or having to drop out of the race. Don't be surprised when you arrive at the store and the socks cost upwards of $10 a pair.

Bring along at least 5 pair of your favorite socks to the race. Take the extra minute or so to switch into a new pair at each exchange. Make sure to dry your feet and also sprinkle some baby powder on them to keep the moisture at a minimum. Lastly, consider sprinkling some powder in your shoes as well.

Sock Recommendations:
- ➢ Thorlos Experia
- ➢ Cool Max
- ➢ Wigwam Ironman

Shorts

Shorts depend on personal preference. Some prefer the traditional running short while others rave about spandex or biker shorts. Either way, be sure to test different pairs on your long runs. Chafing can and will stop you in your tracks.

Consider the type of material: wicking, cotton, blends etc.

Chapter 25

Your Race Strategy

"Success is peace of mind, which is a direct result of self-satisfaction in knowing you did your best to become the best that you are capable of becoming." – John Wooden

The Day Before

The day before the race, concentrate both on drinking and eating, so that you go into the race well hydrated and loaded up with glycogen. Remember that metabolizing all those carbohydrates that you are loading up takes more water than you think. That being said, you don't want to be getting up every hour on the hour during the night to go to the bathroom.

The day before the race starts, a pre-race meeting is usually hosted by Dale Tuck in the evening and is usually held near the Rec. Centre. A big stage will be set up along with tents selling food, gear, and other race paraphernalia. In this meeting, any changes to the course and/or race are made available. Yes, the race can be changed the day before and even the day of the race. Speak to other racers, race coordinators, and be aware of the fact that changes might be made.

If Grande Cache experiences any rain in the days prior to the race, mosquito's could be an issue so bring bug spray and have warm clothes readily available as the meeting is outdoors. You will feel overwhelmed and only want to concentrate on yourself but try your best to be present. Most likely other friends and racers will try to chat with you about how you feel and how your training has gone. Remember, they are as nervous as you are.

All racer's are feeling a little insecure at this point. Most are worried if their training was enough or trying to gain some last minute information that they failed to prepare for before hand. It's natural. It doesn't help that the meeting is held directly in front of the mountains you will be going up the next morning! That being said, you will not be this person. You will have all the answers because you have prepared beforehand. You will walk around confidently knowing that you did everything you could have done in your preparation for the race. This is not the time to discuss race strategies with other racers nor is the time to waste socializing. Get the information you need and head to your hotel room or tent.

Pre Race Dinner

You will receive a race kit upon your arrival, which will include a coupon for a pasta dinner at the Rec Centre. You paid for it so you might as well enjoy it. That being said, some individuals simply don't have the ability to eat a huge pasta dinner the night before a race. Additionally, when digesting pasta it requires water, which is pulled away from your reserves and can dehydrate you throughout the night. Ideally, your training will have prepared you with a list of pre-race dinners that you are comfortable with and know will do the trick. Also, take a high dosage of vitamin C the night before. This will help boost your immunity into the race.

*Hint: avoid foods that are raw and lightly cooked. Salads and fish can wreak havoc if eaten the day before the race. The salad may not be clean, and the fish may not be fully cooked throughout. Avoid stuffing yourself with food or water the night before. A modest meal with easily digested carbohydrates, and some fat usually works well.

The Night and Day Before The Race

The night before the race plays an integral role in your successful completion of the death race. Ideally, you will have prepared and set out everything you need for race day. Having done this will allow you to dismiss thoughts of having anything to do the morning of the race and will help you sleep. Your crew, if you have one, should be prepped and ready. The race day outfit will be set out with care. Pin your race number somewhere on your outfit ahead of time. Remember that pictures are usually taken in the race from the front, so your number should be facing forward rather than on the side. Prepare the hydration pack and its supplies ahead of time. Make sure everything you need is in the right pockets. It helps knowing ahead of time which pockets contain what. Tell your crew as well so when they load the bag at the transitions you will know where things are at during the race.

Weather

During the last week before the CDR, you will be one of the many looking up the weather report. Will it be rainy, humid, dry, wet, cold, hot, etc? The worst part of it all is that the weather can and will change the day before hand. Do not pay attention to the weather until the day before the race! You will already have other things to think and prepare for. Additionally, it will make you more nervous and anxious. Look at it once the evening before the race and plan your strategy appropriately.

The Morning of The Race

Time to wake up! It's race day. I recommend trying to wake up at 5:00 am for a quick hearty breakfast. The breakfast should be eaten at least 1-2 hours before and should be easily digestible, familiar, and high in carbohydrates. Make sure that you have practiced with this pre-race breakfast in training. It should not produce gastrointestinal distress, should be moderate in protein and low in fat. If nerves prevent intake of solids then drink fruit juices, sports drinks or glycogen replacement products.

Examples: bagels, whole wheat bread, crackers, jelly, all juices, brown/white rice, English muffins, cereal, pasta, sports drinks, apples, bananas, oranges, raisins.

DO NOT TRY ANYTHING NEW ON RACE DAY!

This is one of the most commonly broken rules of race preparation. Many runners get psyched out before the race and start think "I need some kind of super food or those high performance gels to get me through this!" They forget, however, that they didn't need any of that crap during their training and completed those runs just fine.

Once your finished, you can try to go back to sleep. If not, your months of preparation and training are finally coming to an end. This is your final exam. Are you ready? Are you beaming with pride and excitement? Yes, your legs are likely to run off without you! Settle down and take a deep breath. Try to relax. This is going to be a long and grueling race. Make sure you apply band-aids and lubricant to the necessary areas.

The pre-race ceremony will start at 7:40 am and the race will start at 8 am. Don't worry about getting there early. Stay off your feet and try to concentrate on your pre-planned strategy. Take a few pictures with your crew and family. You will cherish these photos! You will be a different and changed person from the person you started the race as.

Around 10 minutes before the race wave goodbye to your crew and find a position in the starting line near the middle, as you don't want to get stuck behind the slow pokes! Continue to breath. Your heart is beating hard. Your excited! Control your emotions. Remember the first four miles are the most important, as you will want to conserve your glycogen. The 5:1 run/walk ratio is far more sparing of the body's energy reserves than running 25:5.

Race Day Strategy - A Brief Overview
Overall Strategy: Completion of this race will depend on many things going right and few things going wrong. Pacing, Nutrition, Hydration, Weather, Physical health and Mental health will all be factors. There are 5 legs in total. Be calm and relax. Try to remember your preparation and be confident. Follow the methods you have practiced in training.

•Hydration: Try to consume ~1 liter of hydration per hour and take one succeed cap per hour or two if hot. Monitor your sweating and heart rate. Try to drink every 20 to 30 minutes rather than every hour.

•Nutrition: most of the race will consist of a liquid diet and gels. Start eating solid foods in small increments at later stages of the race. Our bodies cannot absorb more than 300 calories per hour. Shoot for mostly complex carbohydrates with maybe 20% of calories from fats and 10% from proteins.

Key Points:

➤ Do not allow your competitive side to take over too early and or allow yourself to fall out of your game plan. Do not allow others to dictate your race.

➤ During the later stages you will be akin to walking everything. Ask yourself "Is it that I can't run or that I do not want to run." It helps to join other runners. That being said, do not join someone who is going to fast or to slow. It is easy to become joined at the hip with a runner but realize when you need to break off.

➤ Don't forget to enjoy the scenery and or to talk to the other runners you are running with. Also, remember that your crew support doesn't have to be there. Let them know that you are happy to share this experience with them and try your best not to get frustrated with them. Consider getting matching colorful t-shirts for your crew members to make it easy for you to find them and to show them that they are truly needed part of your team.

Chapter 26

Leg Strategies

"Despite what seems like the extraordinary nature of these events, in the end, they make you even more human." - Joel McNamara

Leg 1 Summary: 19 kilometers; 6 kilometers of pavement; 3.5 kilometer of gravel road; elevation loss over 500 feet; race starts in downtown Grande Cache at the Rec Centre before heading onto the highway and into the woods. You will hear and read that this is a relatively easy leg. The key word is relative. It is not easy. DO NOT BELIEVE THE WEBSITE SUMMARY! These are not rolling hills with some flat sections! You will be walking the uphills and some sections. Lastly, use your poles in this section.

Hydration Pack: carry one liter of water and one liter of Hammer Perpeteum (or whatever sports drink you like)

Nutrition: consume one or two gels (solid food comes later)
Shoes: hybrid road/trail runners (i.e. Brooks Cascadia) Poles: YES (you will hear some runners not using them; trust me and use them for your first time)

The gun sounds. Don't forget to start GPS as you shuffle across the starting line. Many of the racers will blast out of the gate. NOT YOU. The pavement feels fast beneath your feet. People will pass you. Let them. Resist the urge to surge. Pacing is extremely important during this section. Remind yourself that many of the front-runners are usually the relay runners and elite racers.

*Hint: start in the middle of the pack somewhere and don't get caught with the slow pokes.

The Course: the first 5 kilometers of pavement includes one slight uphill that you will walk and one long downhill that will be run at a comfortable pace. At the 5-kilometer mark, you double back along the highway on a dirt road that immediately presents you with another slight uphill that you will walk. At 6 kilometers, you hit enter into the woods. This section is mostly mud and single track, which makes passing difficult. Take it easy and save your energy for the gruesome Leg 2. Your mantra for this leg is to conserve, conserve, conserve. Watch the mud and water sections. Take light steps with minimal impact. Use your poles to buffer the downhill's and propel you through the uphill's.

Expected Time: 2 Hours

TRANSITION: take 5 minutes to switch socks and shoes if desired; apply Vaseline or baby powder to your feet; have an extra hydration pack already prepared with 3 liters of water and any mandatory gear.

Leg 2 Summary: 27 kilometers; considered the hardest and most technical leg for soloists; expect long extended ascents and descents through dirt trail, rocks, mud, and water; elevation change of 5,000+ feet; 2 creek crossings; Emergency aid station at 36km.

Hydration Pack: minimum 3 liters of hydration. Half water and half Hammer Perpeteum. Five to seven succeed caps.

Nutrition: consume a gel every other hour or as needed. Take small bag of solid food to munch on if intermittently. Also, carry three extra servings perpeteum to mix.

Shoes: Trail

Poles: YES (no questions asked)

Almost immediately you start a gradual ascent, which you will hike. Use your poles to help on the ascent. Step aside when you feel out of breath or if your legs start to cramp. If the course is wet or the weather is rainy expect nasty trail conditions. Expect cramps and sluggishness due to the altitude and be prepared to deal with it by upping your sodium intake.

*Hint: if you're feeling weak or sluggish take small 30 second breaks on the ascents. Pushing it past your redline won't save that much time and you can make up for them on the descents.

The Course: prepare to ascend Mt Flood, tackle the slugfest and bum slide, and to climb up Mt. Grande. The trail from Flood to Grande is treacherous with several steep drop-offs. You will likely burn through your hydration around the time you reach the emergency aid station at 36 km. Refill your pack and mix the perpeteum. Once you ascend Mt. Flood, it will seem as if the descents and ascents are never coming to an end. Be patient. You will soon finish the leg back at the starting line.

Expected Time: 5 to 6 Hours

TRANSISTION: take 10 minutes to recuperate.

Leg 3 Summary: 23 kilometers; considered the easiest leg and the fastest terrain; first 5 kilometers are pavement and the rest is dirt road; contains sections littered with watermelon size rocks; one knee deep river crossing; expect long sections of trail exposed to heat.

Hydration Pack: 3 liters (Take 3 to be safe)
Nutrition: get some solid foods down and 2 to 3 energy gels
Shoes: Road
Poles: NO (give your arms a break – you will need them for the Mt. Hamel)

You're legs will feel like lead weights after that torturous leg 2. Leg 3 is unanimously voted as the easiest leg, but nothing is easy after having just completed leg 1 and 2. This leg can be tricky. Many perish due to the heat and a lack in hydration.

*Hint: take 3 liters of water. Many expect that this leg, being only 23 kilometers, will take ~2 hours. The added weight will be less of a deterrent than you having to walk the last few kilometers because you ran out of hydration and possibly missing the cutoff.

The Course: start off this leg on an easy 5 km of pavement. Once you hit dirt, a small ascent awaits, but do not fear as an easier jaunt is soon coming. As you leave the pavement, you enter a section of shaded woods that takes your through a rolling terrain of rocks and roots, so mind your step. Once you exit the bush, a mix of logging roads and highways awaits before you reach the aid station before Leg 4.

Expected Time: 2 hours 45 minutes

TRANSITION: take 5 minutes; change socks and shoes if necessary.

Leg 4 Summary: 38 kilometers; longest and 2nd hardest leg for soloists; 10 km sustained ascent up Hamel; beware of the switchbacks; temperatures and humidity could be a factor; one really long runable descent followed by some relatively flat sections going into and out of Ambler aid station.

Hydration Pack: 3 liters
Nutrition: hold off on eating any solids at the transition.
Shoes: Road (you can get away with them and the cushion feels nice)
Poles: YES

*Hint: take it easy on the ascent towards Mt. Hamel and use the runnable descent down to make up some time. The flatter sections following the descent also help provide some relief.

The Course: first 10 km is continuous climbing until you reach the summit of Hamel at 7,000 feet where the air is thin. You will trek the first 4 km through the forest. At the 4 km mark you will have a slight descent where you will immediately start back up again. Beware of the boulders strewn across the switchback before Hamel. Once you summit, a prayer flag awaits. You have to opportunity to drop your pack and then traverse the summit ridge. Grab a prayer flag and return it to one of the race volunteers before starting the long steep descent off of Mt. Hamel. Once down the mountain, you will follow some meandering roads through an area scorched by forest fires and then a 4 km jaunt around Ambler loop. After the Ambler loop, you have approximately 10 km left of runnable logging roads at a slight descent, perfect for a run/walk strategy.

*Hint: At the Ambler loop you are allowed a drop off bag. Use it wisely. Consider changing into some lighter and less technical shoes.

Expected Time: 7 to 8 hours

TRANSITION: take 10 minutes; change socks and shoes if necessary.

Leg 5 Summary: 22 kilometers; most likely run entirely in the Darkness; Oh, those pesky roots!

Hydration Pack: 3 liters
Nutrition: hold off on eating any solids at the transition.
Shoes: Road (you can get away with them and the cushion feels nice)
Poles: YES

*Hint: assuming you have made it into leg 5, try pairing up with a relay runner. Just make sure you let them go first. Not only will the racer keep you company but they will also hit every root, stick, and rock before you do, thereby, alerting you to a potential mishap. It could very easily save you the agony of a black toe or even worse, an race ending fall.

The Course: It starts by going straight up an embankment and into a heavy canopy of trees. The single track trail is easily identifiable and marked exceptionally well, but littered with potential hazards. Oh, those pesky roots! Watch your step. Most are on leg 5 (conveniently the leg is at night), but be careful of the occasional root throughout the rest of the course. The trail eventually exits onto the sulphur gates road across from the Hell's Gates emergency aid station about 5 km from where you started. You will check in and cross the Hell's Gate road and head down a road to the Boat Launch. From there, you will descend down a decline to the river, staying left at the fork. At the river, the reaper will ask for your death race coin. Once you hand it to him, you will climb a small embankment where you will "hop" onto the boat. Be careful to not fall in! You will then be ferried across the Smoky River. The boat will actually drive onto the shore where you will then be expected to jump down, about 4 feet, from the boat. Not an easy feat after having just run 100+ kilometers. From the river comes the "hill that never ends", it is a long climb up to the top of the far side before you disappear into the trees where there is a wider trail but lots of sections with overhanging branches and more roots that can be trickery and slippery.

Expected Time: 3 hours 45 minutes

Chapter 27

Crew Support

"Most people run a race to see who is the fastest. I run a race to see who has the most guts." - Pre Fontaine

Running the Canadian Death Race without crew support is doable. It's not easy and requires extensive preparation, but it's not impossible. This is a long race (obviously) and having a friendly face at each aid station goes a long way in lifting ones spirits. Convince, persuade, and even offer to pay your friends to be your support crew! Offer FREE BEER. Who declines free beer?

If you have been blessed with a support crew then they will need detailed instructions. When I say detailed, I don't mean calling up Mark Smith and saying, "you're in charge of my hydration" and sending an email to Paul Jones indicating, "you're in charge of my food". The more details the better. The job of your support crew is to ensure that you remain adequately hydrated, nourished, physically intact, and geared up, and to get you back into the race as soon as possible.

Have note cards for each crew member. Laminate them. A sample card would look something like this:

Mark Smith
Leg 1: prepare hydration; have shoe replacement ready, pack nutrition; transition time 5 minutes
Leg 2: have socks ready for exchange, have baby powder or body glide out, transition time 10 minutes
Leg 3: switch to running shoes, have food set out, transition time 5 minutes
Leg 4: etc
Leg 5: etc

Crew Rules are important. These are the most important but not all-inclusive. Be sure to check the race brochure for added rules. You would hate to be the one person who gets disqualified at kilometer 82 at the fault of one of your support crew.

CREW RULES
1) Crews are only allowed at any of the full emergency aid stations with the exception of Ambler Loop.

2) Do not park on the highway at any time. All aid stations have plenty of parking at the sites.

3) Crews may only assist within the marked aid stations. No pacing or assisting outside these zones.

4) Aid station food is only for racers on course

5) Water is for hydration only and not for showering purposes

PARKING PASS & DIRECTIONS
When you pick up your race package, there will be a parking pass, which has detailed directions to each aid station for your support crew. On race day, make sure you crew has the pass in their car or they will not be allowed into the aid station. Make sure your crew understands that there will be traffic on race day. Although, there is a significant amount of time between aid stations, parking will take time. Additionally, the car will be parked far away from where the location of the aid station which could make the transportation of your gear, hydration, and food a little more difficult. Carrying the gear from the car, back and forth, could be

tedious so try to pack efficiently and concisely. This is not as big of a deal if you have more than one support crew but if you only have one person, they only have two arms. Make sure they can carry everything you might need on one trip from the car to the aid station

You will receive one parking pass in your race kit. You will get one parking pass per soloist and one per relay team. Have them displayed in the font of your vehicle window or you will be turned away.

Directions To Relay Exchange
Transition Staging areas accessible to support crew

Transition 1/2: Denard Railyard - Hwy 40 S, 10.3 km from Hoppe Ave, dirt road to right, watch for LA PRAIRIE GROUP sign.

Transition 2/3: Start/Finish Line, Downtown - Hoppe Ave in front of Rec Centre

Transition 3/4: Hamel Base, Hwy 40 N, 16.3 km from Hoppe Ave (solo & relay)

Transition 4/5: Sulphur Gates Road - Hwy 40 N, 6.8 km, past the blue bridge just past Sulphur Gates Road to your left. (Cement plant on your right)

Chapter 28

Facebook

"When you're afraid of failure you're more likely to do it." – Gordy Ainsleigh

The Canadian Death Race is much more than a race. Yes, it is a brutally tough beast of a course, but it's also a race where friendships are forged. There is a Facebook group, hosted by Death Race Head Quarter's, where you can interact with other racers. Take advantage of it. This page offers you the chance to ask questions about the course, compare training notes and vent any frustrations. When you're going through the slugfest or summiting Hamel it helps to have fellow racers around. There is nothing more uplifting than a friendly face.

*Hint: read through the past discussions on Facebook to get an idea of other racers have gone through in the past. There is a wealth of information here.

Chapter 29

Awards Ceremony

"The test of any man's character is how he takes praise." – Anonymous

Your have just finished The Canadian Death Race! Congratulations. Now what? First, rest and then recovery! On the Monday following the race, at 8 a.m., an awards ceremony will be held at the Recreation Center. Refreshments and a small selection of eats will be provided at a small price. You will have the chance to view the race video and speak to other racers about your completion as a soloist. Yes, you have bragging rights now! In years prior the cost of the DVD was $25. This preview should last around 15 or 20 minutes. If you have your heart set on taking home a DVD, make sure you get there early. This past year they ran out and were scurrying to copy more to satisfy demand.

The top finishers, as well as, all soloists are usually called to the front to be recognized. This is the time to walk tall. Be proud of what you have just accomplished. You will be recognized for the months of your dedication and hard work. What a feeling! Top finishers will be recognized and then you will be called up on the stage, one by one, to accept your finisher's coin!

Congratulations! Pat yourself on the back.

Stick around for the ceremony if you can! Especially, if you ran the race solo. The last thing you want to do after finishing the race is get on an airplane and/or drive several hours. Yes, spending an extra day costs extra money for a hotel and you're probably tired but try to relax and try to enjoy your tremendous accomplishment.

Additionally, Scott Woodward of Barebones Production usually has a DVD for $25 during the awards ceremony.

Scott Woodward at Barebones Production
dvd@canadiandeathrace.com

Margaret of Photoscapes has pictures for sale for $12/piece. If you're not able to attend, you can send them an email request.
Their contact information is below.

Margaret of Photoscapes - info@photoscapesbymargaret.com

Chapter 30

Post Race Depression

"Tough times don't last, but tough people do." – A.C. Green

Many speak of the "after race blues" following a marathon. Well, you spent more than twice that time training and probably even more in preparation. It's all come to an end! It's not unusual to feel a little bit down. When you're in the middle of training or the race, it was everything. You were being tested to your utmost limits. Now that you finished, having no goals may make life seem small and somewhat insignificant. What do you do now?

Before you start running again, take some time to recover. Take up something else that you love to do. Another hobby. Another passion. Fill your time by hanging out with your friends and family. It's likely in the past months you have showed some neglect in this area due to all the training. Tell your story! People will awe in amazement and wonder how in the world someone can do something like this? It's fun and you have the rights to brag!

Chapter 31

Conclusion

"In that he didn't die at the finish line, he could have run faster." – Tim Noakes

      Competing the Canadian Death Race is an astounding challenge. It will not be easy and will challenge your physical, as well as, mental perseverance.

      Reading through this at first will seem overwhelming. Read different parts in you spare time and break it up into pieces. The training process is always a work in progress. Your journey towards the finish line will have its ups and downs. It's how you get through the times that will see through to the finish line.

Most importantly, remember to have fun! Many forget why they decided to accept the challenge in the first place.

ADDENDUM

RACE DAY BAG
- 5 Pairs of Socks
- Old pair of shoes (to be cut up if needed)
- Shoes: 3 Pairs
- 5 Running Shirts
- Hoodie
- Blanket (old & used) – grab one from the plane
- Sweat Pants
- Jacket
- Extra Hats
- Gloves for Pole Protection
- Umbrella
- Flash Light

RACE DAY OUTFIT – set out ahead of time
- Shoes
- Socks
- Shorts
- Shirt
- Compression Socks
- GPS
- Running Hat
- Hydrations Pack
- Sunscreen & Vaseline
- Sunglasses
- Apply lubricant
- Band-Aids
- Duct Tape
- Coin Case
- MP3 Player

TOOLKIT
- Body Glide/Vaseline/Bag Balm
- Bandaids/Moleskin
- Advil
- Rolaids
- Caffeine
- Toilet Paper
- Headlamps (2-3)
- Safety glasses
- Tape for foot repair (electrical, duct, and sports)
- Hand wipes
- Sunscreen
- Small Scissors
- Bug spray
- Gold Bond
- Pocket Knife

PRE RACE BREAKFAST
- Bagels
- Whole Wheat Bread
- Crackers
- Jelly
- Juice
- Brown & White Race
- English Muffins
- Cereal
- Pasta
- Sports Drinks
- Apples
- Bananas
- Oranges
- Raisins

RACE DAY FOODS
- Boiled Potatoes
- Pretzels
- Peanut Butter
- Espresso Brownies
- Chicken Noodle Soup
- Shredded Chicken
- Potato Chips
- Rice Krispy Treats
- Apricot
- Potato Bread
- Pastrami
- Oatmeal
- Bagel
- Mac & Cheese
- Cookies

COIN CASE
- Death Coin
- Sunscreen
- Salt Tablets
- Advil

HYDRATION PACK
- Medication Kit – Advil, Rolaids, caffeine, Vaseline
- Wind Resistant breaker ✓
- Headlamp ✓
- Toilet Paper
- Extra Socks ✓
- Candy ✓
- Blister Kit
- Duct Tape ✓
- Eye Protection ✓
- Energy Gels ✓
- Gloves
- Hat ✓

Minimum Equipment List:

> Hydration (Water or Electrolyte Solution, All runners)
> Wind and water resistant/proof jacket (All runners)
> Fingered gloves (All runners)
> Insulated headband or insulated hat, or hooded jacket. (All runners)
> Headlamp or flashlight if you will be running during the night. (Night runners*)
> Extra Headlamp
> Clear or light amber eye protection if you will be running during the night. (Night runners*)

* These items required for anyone starting leg 4 after 5pm, or if you will be leaving the Beaver Dam aid station or Hell's gates river crossing after 9:50pm. For your own safety you will not be allowed to continue without these essential items after the 9:50pm cut-off time.

Recommended Equipment List:
(If you choose not to carry these items with you then it is recommended you have them available to you from your crew at each aid station.) - Moleskin, Band-Aids, duct tape - Fanny pack or small backpack - Hydration system (large reservoir) and/or two to three - large water bottles - High-energy food and drink - Long lasting waterproof and sweat proof Sunscreen & lip balm (at 6000 to 7000ft skin burns quite easily even on a cloudy day) - Vaseline - Sunglasses (anti-fog with good ventilation lens work best) - Rain Gear - Use a layering system for your clothing. - Extra running shoes & socks - Headlamp - Extra Batteries - Bear Bangers and/or Bear Spray

RULES

➤ You may not stash gear, food or water along the course

➤ You must wear all race numbers provided so it is visible and unaltered.

➤ Dropping out - any competitor that drops out of the race must notify the nearest race course marshal at the earliest opportunity, and surrender their coin (and timing stick) Do not drop out of the race without telling race officials; otherwise we will send someone to look for you. There is nothing worse than having a frantic search for a lost racer take place while that person is having a beer in one of the patios downtown. If you drop out then please tell us. 8. Race officials may remove any racer from the race course if, in their opinion, it is unsafe for the racer to proceed (e.g. In cases of hypothermia, dehydration, frostbite or other debilitating injury or dangerous wildlife on the trail).

➤ You must wear ID bracelet provided. - acts as a hospital bracelet in the event of emergency.

➤ All Racers must check-in with the timing station at the start of their relay legs. Make sure you arrive at the relay exchange point in plenty of time to do this. Every year at least 3 (sometimes more) teammates show up late to a very choked relay racer who has run their heart out and has been waiting to exchange their coin with them but they are late, sometimes by as much as a half an hour.

➤ All racers must show their Death Race coin at the relay exchange zones, and the summit of each mountain if requested by race marshals. The coin is given to Charon (the ferryman of the dead) at the river crossing in exchange for safe passage across Hell's Gates.

➤ Upon reaching the summit of Hamel you must check in at the Forestry cabin with race volunteers. You will then be instructed to run along the spine of Hamel and retrieve your summit flag at the cliff bluffs above Hell's canyon. You must return to the Forestry cabin with your summit flag as proof of having attained the turnaround point. Details to follow on race day at the race briefing Friday night.

96

➢ You may not loiter at the Hamel Forestry cabin for any reason other than to check-in with race marshals and to turn in your summit flag. Seeking the shelter of the cabin for any period of time will disqualify a racer. The Hamel Hut is intended as an emergency shelter only for rescue purposes

➢ Death Racers on course may help other Death Racers.

➢ No Littering

➢ During the highway sections racers may not run on the pavement of the Highway, you must stay in the ditch and follow the quad track. Racers may only cross the highway at designated marshaled locations when safe to do so. Watch for traffic, the highway is not closed.

➢ Clear lens eye protection for the night section of the race must be worn. The night portion of the race (leg 5) goes through dense forest; eye protection is a must – you will need it. Any runners leaving the Beaver Dam aid station (at HWY 40) after 9:50pm must wear clear, or light amber eye protection, and a headlamp/flashlight in order to continue. Any Runners leaving the Hamel Aid Station (start of leg 4) after 5pm will require a headlamp.

➢ Any runners leaving the Hell's Gate river crossing after 9:50pm also must wear clear, or light amber eye protection, and a headlamp/flashlight in order to continue. Useable daylight hours in early summer are from 5:30am to 10:45pm

➢ All cut off times must be respected, if you didn't make a cut off time you are in over your head and your Timing Stick will not beep when attempting to punch in. If this occurs, we'll see you next year (see section on cutoff times). Surrender your timing stick and coin to race officials.

➢ Equipment drop off at the Ambler Loop Emergency aid station: Runners may elect to have a small bag of equipment and food items sent to this emergency aid station, which will be attended by volunteers only. If you wish to drop off a small equipment bag (ex. headlamp, rain gear, extra food and drink) at the Ambler loop emergency aid station, your drop bag must be clearly marked with your race number on the outside. We recommend something durable and waterproof, at least as strong as double bagged plastic, with race number printed in waterproof black marker on large white tape. All drop bags must be delivered to the drop off at race registration by 8pm Friday evening (penalty box at the hockey rink). Bags can be collected Sunday in the afternoon and Monday at the Awards presentation.

➤ Warning - you may only insert your timing stick once into any check station. Listen for two beeps/two flashes then remove your timing stick from the check station. NO DOUBLE-DIPPING! You may not insert your timing stick again in the same station. This will invalidate your timing file and result in disqualification.

➤ No dousing yourself with water at the aid stations. They are for drinking ONLY.

TRAINING SCHEDULE

Week	Mon	Tues	Wed	Thur	Fri	Sat	Sun	Total
1								
2								
3								
4								
5								
6								
7								
8								
9								
10								
11								
12								
13								
14								
15								
16								
17								
18								
19								
20								
21								
22								

TRAINING SCHEDULE...Continued

Week	Mon	Tues	Wed	Thur	Fri	Sat	Sun	Total
23								
24								
25								
26								
27								
28								
29								
30								

MY TRAINING NOTES

MY TRAINING NOTES

MY TRAINING NOTES

MY TRAINING NOTES

MY TRAINING NOTES

MY TRAINING NOTES
_____

1) Contacls ✓ — John
2. Sunscreen ✓ — Goo L
   — sncreen
3) Glide ✓ — bug spry
   — vaselne
4) Vaseln - feet — biofreeze
5) hat L — shues ✓
   — poles ✓

6) Gamin L
7. Race #
8. wristbond ✓
9. fingerband ✓
10- Put batteres
    in headlamp

8251265R0

Made in the USA
Lexington, KY
22 January 2011